Finland Travel Guide

Captivating Adventures through Must-See Places, Local Culture, Finnish Landmarks, Hidden Gems, and More

Finland Travel Guide

Captivating Adventures through Must-See Places, Local Culture, Finnish Landmarks, Hidden Gems, and More

Welcome Aboard, Discover Your Limited-Time Free Bonus!

Hello, traveler! Welcome to the Captivating Travels family, and thanks for grabbing a copy of this book! Since you've chosen to join us on this journey, we'd like to offer you something special.

Check out the link below for a FREE Ultimate Travel Checklist eBook & Printable PDF to make your travel planning stress-free and enjoyable.

But that's not all - you'll also gain access to our exclusive email list with even more free e-books and insider travel tips. Well, what are you waiting for? Click the link below to join and embark on your next adventure with ease.

Access your bonus here:
https://livetolearn.lpages.co/checklist/
Or, Scan the QR code!

Table of Contents

Introduction

You've taken the first step toward going on an immersive exploration of Finland by choosing this guidebook as your travel companion. While you can find numerous travel guides providing travel-related information, this comprehensive handbook takes you deep into the diverse experiences that define Finland.

From exploring the dynamic urban hubs like Helsinki and Turku to the unspoiled expanses of Lapland, this book has it all. Far beyond a mere manual, this is your key to understanding the nuanced charm and authenticity that sets Finland apart. The country is a prime example of a region where the modern pulse of cities effortlessly blends with nature, each region telling its unique tale of history, tradition, and cultural richness.

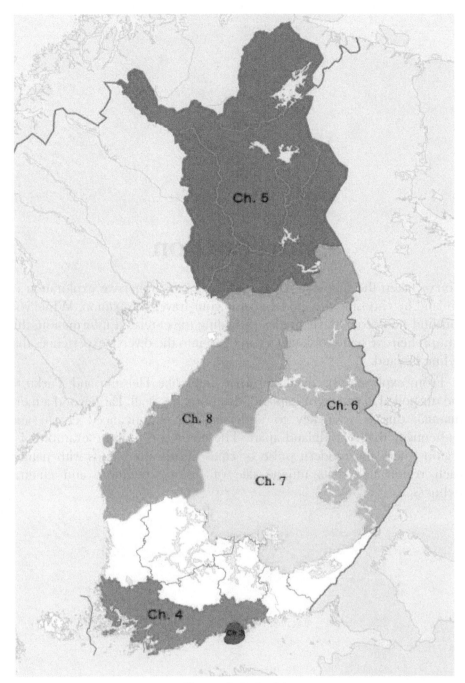

Chapters in the book.[1]

Made for both first-timers and seasoned travelers, this guide takes you through Finland's landscapes, accommodations, dining, and attractions. It leaves no stone unturned. Explore each region and uncover the distinctive character of cities such as Helsinki, Turku, Tampere, and beyond. From iconic landmarks to offbeat discoveries, this guide provides you with the correct information to develop an in-depth understanding of Finland's multifaceted allure. You will find that its well-organized structure makes navigating a wealth of information very easy, allowing you to focus on the substance without feeling overwhelmed.

Throughout the book, you'll also find fascinating facts about the attractions, landmarks, and popular places of interest. Beyond the tourist spots, this guide uncovers opportunities for genuine cultural immersion. From participating in local festivals to experiencing traditional Finnish rituals, it provides avenues for travelers to engage deeply with Finland's cultural tapestry. Each chapter has an experiences section where you can learn more about the culture, traditions, and events that connect you with the roots of the land. Explore Finland's culinary landscape with information on local gastronomy. Discover hidden eateries favored by locals, savor regional specialties, and learn about the cultural significance of Finnish cuisine.

The book also contains a bonus chapter on common expressions and phrases you can practice for better communication and to improve your travel experience. Finland Travel Guide transcends its role as a book and becomes a companion for a rich, immersive exploration through Finland's captivating landscapes and vibrant culture.

Chapter 1: Get to Know Finland

This chapter will cover everything you need to know about Finland. You'll learn about the country's terrain and geographic location. You'll also gain insight into Finland's historical background and its arts, literature, and architecture. You'll find interesting facts about the country and its people, learn about its most popular sports and leisurely activities, and get a taste of Finnish cuisine.

You'll even find a section that gives you just about everything you need to know before you embark on your trip. Finally, you'll learn about the country's transportation systems and the most efficient ways to get around. If you're still unsure about visiting Finland, you're guaranteed to find yourself booking your ticket before you reach the end of this chapter!

Finland's Geographic Location

Finland is located in Northern Europe, with Russia to its east, Norway to its north, and Sweden and the Gulf of Bothnia bordering it on the west. It is considered a geographically remote nation, one-third of which falls in the southern area of the Arctic Circle, which explains its harsh weather conditions. Finland is also mostly covered in woodlands, earning it the title "the continent's most heavily forested nation."

Finland's geographic location.[2]

The country is also home to several rivers, vast marshlands, and a whopping 188,000 lakes, ten of which are over 100 square miles in area. Needless to say, the scenery is like nothing you've seen before. The breathtaking experience starts as soon as your plane crosses the Finnish borders.

The land from above looks surreal! Water and greenery meet wherever your eyes fall. Finland is also characterized by its beautiful mountainous terrain in the northwest, almost serving as a natural physical border with Sweden and Norway. If you're a hiking enthusiast, you'll be happy to learn that the country's highest mountain, Mount Halti, stands at 4,344 feet and can be found in this mountain range.

Natural Attractions

If you're more of a beach person, Finland is also a swimmer's paradise. The country's coastline extends over 2,760 miles. If you go southwest, you'll find numerous islands, 178,947 to be exact!

If you like skiing, you guessed it: Finland also happens to be the place for you. Whether you're interested in wildlife or not, you'll have a great time exploring Finland's natural wonders. You can go birdwatching and spot pied wagtails, eagles, and Siberian jays. You'll also find waterfowl, arctic tern, and black-backed gulls. When exploring the woodland, you'll come across Finnish elk, wolves, bears, lynx, and much more. If you're planning to immerse yourself in nature, brushing up on your wildlife knowledge before your trip will make your adventure even more exciting. On top of all of that, you may even catch the Northern Lights. It truly is a dream destination.

Finland's winter.[3]

If you're not used to the cold, you may want to avoid Finland during the winter. The country, especially the north, experiences extremely harsh and long winters. It can get as cold as −22 °F. On the bright side, if you want to get the full Finnish experience without freezing, the snow never melts on the northern mountain slopes. The temperature also reaches as high as 80 °F in Finland's short summer. The temperature in the southern part of Finland is often around 10 degrees higher than in the north. If you wish to enjoy your stay and cross all those "want-to-do" activities off your Finnish bucket list, you should consider which type of weather best aligns with your preferences.

Languages

There are two national languages in Finland – Finnish and Swedish – making the country officially bilingual. Around 87% of the nation are Finnish speakers, and they mainly occupy the coastal areas and the nation's islands. The government has implemented laws that ensure the fair treatment and provision of rights to both Finnish and Swedish-speaking individuals. A minority of Finnish people also speak Russian and Estonian, and an even smaller population (located in the north) speaks three of the 11 Sami languages.

Historical Background

Starting in the 12th century, Finland was under Swedish rule until it became ruled by a Russian Grand Duke in 1809. The country finally earned its independence in 1917 on account of the Russian Revolution. In the 1940s, however, the nation lost around 11% of its area when a large part of southeast Karelia and the Petsamo area were ceded to the Soviet Union. These areas now belong to Russia.

For the most part, during the Cold War, Finland was able to maintain a neutral stance and emerge unharmed. Their treaty with the Soviet Union, however – which was signed in 1948 and terminated in 1991 – required them to repel any attacks attempted by Germany and its allies through their national territory on the Soviet Union's side. Finland became a part of the UN in 1955 and started working on boosting its trade and building cultural and political relations with other nations. It also started actively representing itself in the Nordic Council.

The Conference on Security and Cooperation held in Europe in 1975 earned the country the recognition it deserved. More people grew aware of Finland's international activities, leading to the Helsinki Accords, which declared that participating nations must recognize the existing borders of European countries and refrain from altering them through military means. The Helsinki Accords also declared that participating nations must avoid intervening in the international affairs of sovereign nations. That said, Finland wasn't a full member of the European Union until 1995. The country has had excellent relations with the neighboring Scandinavian countries for years. They engage in free labor and partake in collaborative scientific, economic, and cultural projects.

Literature, Arts, and Architecture

Artists, architects, and writers naturally took inspiration from their magnificent surroundings. Finland's abundant water sources and its rich forests and woodlands are clear influences on the creative population's work. Elias Lönnrot's "The Kalevala," which is regarded as Finland's national epic, was crucial to the development of a national identity following the independence in 1917. The epic tells the story of the creation of Earth, incorporating elements of Finnish scenery through the use of ballads and incantations that were a part of the Finnish oral tradition.

Albert Edelfelt.'

Alvar Aalto, a renowned Finnish architect, is celebrated for his designs that blended seamlessly with Finland's natural landscape. The Villa Mairea, an example of his modernist work, shows how he used organic shapes and materials to showcase harmony with nature. Albert Edelfelt, a prominent Finnish painter during the 19th and 20th centuries, also heavily features Finnish nature in his paintings. Akseli Gallen-Kallela's works were also inspired by themes from the Kalevala.

Jean Sibelius, one of the most celebrated Finnish composers, created symphonies that were inspired by Finnish folklore and landscapes. Finlandia, a tone poem for orchestra, one of Sibelius' best-known works, is a prime example of this influence. Eino Leno and Edith Södergran frequently expressed their deep connection to nature in their poetry. These are only a few examples of how Finland has inspired influential figures from different artistic disciplines over the years.

Widespread Faiths

With the rise of Christianity and the ongoing crusades in Europe, the religion made its way into Finland in the 13th century. As of today, Finland is one of Europe's most homogeneously Christian nations. The percentage of those with church memberships is also the highest in Scandinavia. While only a relative minority regularly attend church, most live their lives (from baptism to marriage to burial) with the blessing of the church. Most Finns' beliefs relate to the Evangelical Lutheran Church of Finland.

The Orthodox Church of Finland.[5]

The church initially started as an official state church and gradually transitioned into a national one. The Orthodox Church of Finland is the only other denomination with a national church, with a minority of Finns belonging to it. A small religious group relates to the Pentecostal church, and an even smaller group are members of the Roman Catholic Church and independent Protestant churches. There have also been Muslim and Jewish communities living in Finland since the 19th century. At the time, Finland was among the rare places within the Russian Empire where people could freely practice their religion. Finnish Jews were officially granted their rights in 1918, and a few years later, in 1925, the nation established its first Islamic congregation and was the first European country to do so. Around 34% of the Finnish population's religious beliefs are not clearly stated.

Interesting Facts about Finland and Finns

It's the World's Happiest Country

Did you know that as of the date of this book's printing, Finland has been named "the happiest country in the world" for *seven consecutive years*? The World Happiness Report is released annually by the UN and takes into account factors such as GDP per capita, level of corruption, average life expectancy, generosity, freedom to make decisions, and much more. It's a holistic measure of a population's happiness.

The scenery and natural environment are likely major contributing factors to Finnish happiness levels. Being surrounded by nature is scientifically proven to lower stress and anxiety levels and promote positivity, joy, and relaxation. Being surrounded by nature also boosts creativity and concentration, enhancing productivity and, therefore, improving one's sense of self and sense of achievement. Additionally, Finland offers incredible education and free healthcare, providing one of the best healthcare systems in the world. The Finnish people are generally inclined toward leading healthy lifestyles. They eat healthy diets and have fun prioritizing their mental and physical health. As you read this book, you'll learn more about the variety of entertainment options that the country has to offer, prompting its residents to enjoy life to the fullest.

There Are State-Funded Maternity Boxes and Gifts

Serving as a testament to Finland's exemplary welfare system, the state offers a fully-funded maternity box to each expecting mother. This gift includes everything that a soon-to-be-mother will need to care for her newborn baby. This box not only offers baby products, mattresses, blankets, snow suits, towels, mittens, personal care items, toys, a wide range of clothes, and nearly everything that might cross your mind, but it also doubles as a perfectly safe crib. This tradition has been going strong for over 8 decades, likely contributing to the country's lowest infant

mortality rate ranking in the world.

Speeding Tickets Are Income-Based

The Finnish government prioritizes its people's welfare, and speeding fines are primarily determined based on the culprit's income. The responsible entity estimates the offender's daily disposable income and how fast they were going above the speed limit. While this is a relief for lower- and middle-class individuals, it means that multimillionaires can be fined A LOT! In the summer of 2023, a driver was fined $194,694 for speeding!

Finland Hosts Some of the Weirdest Competitions

You'll never feel bored in Finland because it happens to be home to one of the world's weirdest competitions. Surprisingly, one of the nation's most popular competitions is the "Wife Carrying World Championship." Just as the name implies, men have to carry their wives, girlfriends, or even female friends through an obstacle course. The first one to complete the course wins. The prize is even more bizarre! Whoever wins gets as much beer in liters as the woman weighs in kilos.

The "Air Guitar World Championship" is equally fascinating. This competition gathers participants from all corners of the world who compete in air guitar playing. If you think that this doesn't require much talent, wait until you find out that they started organizing pre-qualifiers as the competition started growing extremely popular.

Finns Are Heavy Coffee Drinkers

If you think you're a heavy coffee drinker, you'll be relieved to learn about the amount of coffee that an average Finnish adult consumes a day. If there was a global ranking for most cups of coffee consumed, Finland would be first on that list. According to the International Coffee Organization, their annual statistics have revealed that an average Finn drinks around 26.45 lbs. of coffee a year, which is the equivalent of five to eight cups a day. The reason why they consume so much coffee can be explained, to some extent, by their culture. They enjoy this beverage to warm up, stay awake when the sun sets very early in the day when hanging out with friends, or even on their way to the sauna.

There Are Over Three Million Saunas in the Country

For a population of only 5.5 million, having over three million saunas is shocking. In Finnish culture, saunas are perceived as a place to cleanse and relax the mind and body. It boosts mental, emotional, physical, and social health, serving as a holistic healing experience. Finns go there to unwind from the stresses of everyday life, meet up with their friends, socialize, and get to know new people. Further emphasizing how important saunas are to the population, they're not uncommon to find in diplomatic establishments, workplaces, student accommodations, homes, and gyms.

Finland Is Known for Its Metal Bands

Heavy metal has always been stereotyped as carrying negative emotions and having themes associated with violence, aggression, and depression. Finns, however, are here to change this widespread stereotype. Finland carries records for both being the happiest country in the world and having a staggering ratio of 70.6 heavy metal bands per 100,000 national residents (the highest in the world), proving that joy and this music genre can coexist. Unsurprisingly, many world-renowned heavy metal bands like Nightwish, Lordi, and Apocalypta are Finnish. To further show how popular heavy metal is in Finland, some bands, like Hevisaurus, who dress up as dinosaurs, make metal music for kids.

They Invented the "Sisu" Culture

The word "Sisu" can't be accurately translated into the English language. It's a concept that Finns have lived by and incorporated into their lives for centuries. In essence, "Sisu" is the ability to stay determined and strong even when things get tough. They always aim to persevere and push themselves through challenges until they successfully complete their tasks and goals. They do whatever it takes to get things done and take accountability for their actions and decisions, even when they backfire. They own everything they do, decide, and say with courage and stick with it until the very end. That is why Finland always comes out on top. Their culture encourages them to try their hardest even when they doubt they'll succeed.

Famous Sports and Leisurely Activities in Finland

Ice hockey is the most popular game in Finland. Not only is it watched and enjoyed on a large scale, the Finnish men's ice hockey team won first place at both the 2022 World Championship and Olympics. Some of the highest-ranked players in the North American NHL, like Jari Kurri and Teemu Selänne, along with rising stars like Aleksander Barkov and Mikko Rantanen, are Finnish.

Finland celebrating the 2022 World Championship.[6]

Local large-scale competitions like Liiga, or more commonly known as the Finnish Elite League, are also held regularly, garnering an incredibly high viewership. Ice hockey brings the population together. People get together to watch the game and celebrate their favorite team's wins by gathering in market squares. They even take it as far as jumping in fountains (even when it's cold) to express their joy. Athletics and soccer come after ice hockey on the most popular sports list. Apart from watching hockey, most Finns spend their free time reading, walking, or cycling. In winter, you'll find many people skiing and skating outside.

Finnish Cuisine

Finnish cuisine is naturally inspired by the country's geographical situation. Seafood is very popular in Finland, overlooking the Baltic Sea. It is the star component in numerous traditional dishes. Finland's climate and terrain are also ideal for growing root vegetables, making them key ingredients as well. The nation's history also significantly influences its cuisine. Finnish food is a fusion of Swedish and Russian cuisine – and that of other countries in the region.

Finns also mostly smoke, pickle, and salt their food. Since produce is not always available during prolonged winters, Finnish people traditionally used these methods to preserve their food. During the summer, dishes are always enriched with seasonal vegetables and berries. There are also traditional dishes for every special occasion and holiday, like Christmas, incorporating casseroles and ham, and Midsummer, including sausages and fish.

Finnish food is generally very light, healthy, and is made of locally sourced ingredients. If you're into fresh dishes, you'll enjoy the high quality and simple yet flavorful touches of Finnish cuisine. Upon your visit, make sure you try Karjalanpiirakka, which are delicious potato or rice-filled pastries, Graavilohi, an incredible fusion of sweet and savory cured salmon, and Lihapullat, which are special Finnish meatballs.

Things to Know Before Visiting Finland

The Seasons Will Either Make or Break Your Trip

This point is worth mentioning again! Each season in Finland comes with an entirely different yet equally charming experience. In summer, you'll get to enjoy the pleasant climate, go for a dip, and experience the "Midnight sun" if you visit between mid-May and mid-August. During this time, the sun barely sets in northern Finland. Keep in mind that the temperature during summer can get as low as 64 and as high as 80 degrees Fahrenheit, so make sure you pack a wide selection of clothes.

If you plan on visiting during the winter, you can go skiing and even ride a reindeer sleigh. Make sure to go to visit the Arctic Circle's Santa Claus Village, too. That said, it's not all magical. There are sometimes horrible blizzards in winter, especially in the north.

You Don't Need to Learn the Language

English is widespread in Finland and is spoken fluently by many locals, especially in urban areas. You can travel around and explore the country without worrying about the language barrier.

You Don't Need to Tip

There are many countries around the world where tipping is not only a common practice but highly expected of you. That isn't the case in Finland. Bills generally include a service fee, and staff are usually paid decent wages. Unlike the USA, for instance, their income doesn't heavily rely on tips.

You'll Have to Plan If You Want to See the Northern Lights

You likely won't catch the Northern Lights by coincidence. Catching this aurora requires some planning, but it's undeniably worth the effort. To see the Northern Lights, you'll have to visit the country any time between September and March. You'll also have to head out north to Lapland, as you won't be able to see the phenomenon from the city. Rovaniemi is the most popular place to go to see the lights. To avoid any disappointments, you must know that seeing the Northern Lights isn't guaranteed. Most people have to spend a few days in the area before they can catch a glimpse due to the aurora's elusive nature.

You Likely Wouldn't Have to Drive

If you're going to be mostly staying in the country's urban areas, you'll easily get the hang of using public transport. From trams and trains to public buses, Finland's transportation systems are highly efficient, reliable, and easy to use. These systems are well-connected, ensuring that you'll get exactly where you need to be on time. If you want to cut down your travel costs, it would be a great idea to get a Helsinki Card or purchase a travel pass.

You Don't Need Heaps of Cash

Finland, for the most part, is a cashless country. You can use credit and debit cards for everything, even the smallest transactions. While it would still be wise to have some cash on you in case of emergencies or if something goes wrong, you don't need to worry about getting a lot of cash and exchanging currency.

Familiarize Yourself with Cultural Etiquette and the Finnish Personality

Finns are generally reserved in nature. They deeply value their privacy and personal space and are used to keeping a comfortable distance even in social gatherings. When interacting with Finns, be careful not to overstep their boundaries and avoid making them feel uncomfortable. Finnish people are very polite and friendly. However, don't expect them to make small talk or engage in useless long conversations. While they might seem uptight to strangers, they are enjoyable to be around and make amazing friends once you get to know them. They are also very modest; you'll seldom find anyone going on about their personal achievements. They also usually don't know how to respond to compliments and praise.

It's a Very Expensive Country

If you compare the prices in Finland to other places in the world, you'll find that it's relatively expensive. The government does an excellent job of providing top-tier services to the population. This, however, means that taxes are quite high. This is not a significant problem for most Finns because salaries are typically high, and that makes up for this issue. Tourists, on the other hand, will likely find it expensive. While this may seem off-putting, it should not discourage you from visiting the country. Finland is breathtaking and definitely worth experiencing at least once in a lifetime.

Guide to Finland's Transportation

Finland's public transportation system is very organized and punctual. There are continuously updated schedules for each mode of transportation detailing where it is going, departure times, arrival times, and so on. Be careful when checking the timetables because they vary frequently, especially during the holidays, weekends, and with the changing seasons. Most people learn this the hard way, so keep in mind that presenting an incorrect or invalid ticket can result in an 80-euro fine. If you're traveling to Finland for educational purposes, you may be eligible for discounts on season tickets.

Buses

The bus is among the most popular and most accessible transportation systems in the country. This mode of transportation is suitable for both long and short trips. You can rely on them for safety and punctuality. If you're an international undergraduate student, you'll get a discount on tour trips by presenting your Finnish student card. Buses in Finland are relatively comfortable. They are also equipped with free Wi-Fi.

Trains

If you're seeking a more comfortable option, you can opt for trains. They are significantly faster than buses and are highly convenient. They are also a better option for long trips because they have private sleeping cabins, food, and drink. Inter-city trains are also equipped with a children's play area. If you're traveling with kids, you'll no longer have to hear the words, "Are we there yet?" Students with valid Finnish student cards are also eligible for discounts on their train rides.

Bicycles

Bicycles are among the most popular means of transportation in Finland, especially in urban areas during summer. Finns use bikes to run errands, go to work or school, and get some outdoor exercise. Many tourists also use bikes to explore the country. It's an efficient way to move around while enjoying the scenic landscapes. There are several bike rental services available in different areas. You can also register in the city bike systems, ask if your accommodation offers bikes, or use specialized apps that help you locate and rent bikes.

Electric Scooters

Electric scooters are another convenient and sustainable way to get around Finland. There are several electric scooter rental services available around Finnish cities that rent to anyone over 12 years old. You can generally go about 40 km before having to stop to charge it.

Ferries

Even if this may not be your go-to mode of transportation during your stay, you have to get on a ferry or a water taxi at least once. While these are available throughout the entire year, they're more popular during the summer – for obvious reasons. Ferries often offer onboard entertainment as well.

Airplanes

While these may not be the most economical travel options, they are certainly the fastest way to get around. Several airlines offer flights inside the country.

Cars

If you decide to rent a car, you'll be able to drive in Finland if you have a valid International Driving Permit. If you're traveling on your own, without the help of a local or a travel agency, this is the best way to visit rural areas.

Whether you're looking for a getaway in a natural environment, want to immerse yourself in the world of history and arts, need a beach holiday, or are searching for an unforgettable Christmas adventure, you're guaranteed to have the time of your life in Finland. With its diverse landscapes and range of activities that vary with the changing seasons, from winter wonderland to summer paradise, the land of a thousand lakes falls nothing short of breathtaking.

Chapter 2: To and From the Airport

When you go to Finland, you'll likely land at the vibrant Helsinki-Vantaa Airport (HEL), the country's primary international gateway and the largest airport in Finland. This bustling hub is more than a transit point. It's also a testament to Finland's efficiency and hospitality.

Helsinki-Vantaa Airport Overview

Size and Significance

Helsinki-Vantaa Airport stands as the key entry point for visitors to Finland, and its significance extends beyond national borders. As the largest airport in the country, it plays a pivotal role in connecting Finland with the global community.

Helsinki-Vantaa Airport.[7]

Layout and Terminals

The airport is meticulously designed, with two main terminals: Terminal 1 (T1) and Terminal 2 (T2). T1 primarily serves European flights and some long-haul routes, while T2 caters to a broader range of international flights. Each terminal boasts modern architecture and streamlined facilities.

Services and Facilities

Helsinki-Vantaa Airport is not just a transportation hub; it's also a destination in and of itself. The airport offers a plethora of services and facilities to ensure the comfort and convenience of travelers. You can relax in style at one of the airport's lounges, which provides a serene atmosphere, refreshments, and business amenities.

The airport houses a diverse range of shops, from Finnish design boutiques to international brands. The dining options mirror Finland's culinary excellence, offering a mix of traditional and global cuisine.

Amenities like baggage services, currency exchange, and medical facilities are also available, ensuring your journey is as seamless as possible. You can stay connected with the airport's free Wi-Fi service, enabling you to catch up on emails, share travel moments, or plan the next leg of your trip.

Airport Transportation Guide

Arriving at or departing from Helsinki-Vantaa Airport (HEL), you can opt for a variety of transportation options.

Taxis

Taxis are readily available at designated taxi ranks just outside both terminals.

Estimated Fare: The journey from the airport to Helsinki city center typically costs €35, with variations based on the time of day and potential additional charges for luggage.

Taxis can be hailed on the spot or pre-booked through various taxi companies and popular ride-sharing apps. It's advisable to check the displayed fare information in the taxi before starting the journey.

Buses

Helsinki-Vantaa Airport is well-connected to the city and surrounding regions through an extensive public bus network. Multiple bus services operate from the airport, serving various destinations. Bus 615 and 620, for example, connect the airport to the city center, offering a cost-effective option. You must plan your route and know about the exact bus numbers for destinations if you are planning to use public bus services.

Buses operate regularly, with a schedule that accommodates both daytime and evening arrivals. The frequency varies, with buses departing every 10 to 30 minutes, depending on the service. Tickets can be purchased from the driver, at ticket machines located at the airport, or via mobile apps. It's worth noting that certain regional travel cards and the Helsinki Card are valid for bus travel from the airport.

This card has been exclusively created for tourists and visitors who want to visit popular attractions and explore the region without breaking the bank. It can be bought from retail shops at the airport and in the city.

Trains

Helsinki-Vantaa Airport has a railway station, providing a swift connection to the city center and other destinations. The I and P trains connect the airport to the Helsinki Central Railway Station, offering a convenient and efficient mode of transport. Trains operate at regular intervals, with departures every 10 to 30 minutes. The journey to the city center takes approximately 30 minutes. Train tickets can be purchased from ticket machines at the airport or online. Travel cards, including the Helsinki Card, are generally accepted.

Car Rentals

A range of international and local car rental companies operate at the airport, providing the flexibility of self-driven transportation. It's best to book your rental car in advance online to secure the best rates. Rental counters are located in the arrival halls of both terminals. As the region has a sophisticated road network, opting for a rental can provide the freedom to explore and travel to fit your own arrangements.

Ride-Sharing Services

Ride-sharing services may operate at Helsinki-Vantaa Airport. Major international services like Uber may be available. If you're using ride-sharing services, make sure you have the respective app installed on your phone. Fares may vary based on demand and time of day.

Whether you choose the convenience of a taxi, the cost-effectiveness of public transportation, or the flexibility of a rental car, Helsinki-Vantaa Airport provides a wide array of transportation options tailored to your preferences and travel plans. Guarantee yourself a smooth journey by selecting the mode of transport that best suits your needs.

Exploring the Surrounding Area of Helsinki-Vantaa Airport

For travelers finding themselves with a layover or unexpected delays at Helsinki-Vantaa Airport (HEL), the surrounding area offers a variety of hotels, attractions, and points of interest to make the most of your time. Here's a guide to nearby options for those seeking to explore the surrounding area.

Hotels Near the Airport

Helsinki-Vantaa Airport hosts several hotels catering to various preferences and budgets, ensuring a comfortable stay for short durations.

Name	Information	Address
GLO Hotel Helsinki Airport	Located right at the airport, GLO Hotel offers modern amenities, convenience, and a stylish atmosphere for travelers looking for a seamless stay.	Terminaali, Lentoasemantie, 01530 Vantaa
Hilton Helsinki Airport	Connected to the airport via a covered walkway, Hilton provides luxurious accommodations with excellent facilities, making it an ideal choice for brief stays.	Lentajankuja 1, 01530 Vantaa
Helsinki Airport	A short shuttle ride away, Scandic offers a cozy stay with contemporary design, fitness facilities, and a restaurant.	Lentajantie 1, 01530 Vantaa

Attractions and Points of Interest

Name	Information	Address
Jumbo Shopping Center	A short distance from the airport, Jumbo Shopping Center is one of Finland's largest shopping centers. Here, you can indulge in retail therapy, explore various dining options, and catch a movie.	Vantaanportinkatu 3, 01510 Vantaa
Flamingo Entertainment Center	Connected to Jumbo, Flamingo offers a diverse range of entertainment, including a spa, bowling, a water park, and numerous restaurants. It's an excellent option for families seeking leisure activities.	Tasetie 8, 01510 Vantaa
Aviapolis Business Park	For business travelers, Aviapolis Business Park, situated near the airport, provides opportunities for networking, conferences, and business-related activities.	Ayritie 16-24, 01510 Vantaa
Nuuksio National Park	If you have a more extended layover and a penchant for nature, Nuuksio National Park is just a short drive away. Enjoy the serene Finnish wilderness with walking trails, lakes, and an opportunity to reconnect with nature.	Nuuksiontie 84, 02820 Espoo

| Helsinki City Center | A quick train ride from the airport opens up the possibility of exploring Helsinki's city center. Discover iconic landmarks such as Senate Square, Helsinki Cathedral, and the bustling Market Square. | |

Tips for Layovers

If you have checked baggage, check whether it can be stored at the airport or your chosen hotel to make exploration more convenient.

Use public transportation, taxis, or ride-sharing services to explore nearby attractions. The well-connected railway station and bus services make it easy to navigate.

Before venturing out, explore the amenities within the airport. Lounges, shopping, and dining options provide a comfortable environment to relax during layovers.

Whether you choose to unwind in a nearby hotel, explore shopping and entertainment centers, or venture into the natural beauty of Finland, the surrounding area of Helsinki-Vantaa Airport offers various options to make your layover or unexpected delay a memorable and enjoyable experience.

Airports to Know in Finland

Name	Information	Transport Options
Turku Airport (TKU) - Southwest Finland	Approximately 8 kilometers to the north of Turku city center, Turku Airport serves Southwest Finland.	Taxi services are readily available, offering a convenient and swift journey to the city center. Additionally, public buses connect the airport to various parts of Turku, providing an economical option for travelers.

Tampere-Pirkkala Airport (TMP) - Pirkanmaa region	Tampere-Pirkkala Airport is situated around 13 kilometers southwest of Tampere city center, serving the Pirkanmaa region.	Taxis and rental cars are easily accessible at the airport, providing a straightforward journey to Tampere. For those preferring public transportation, buses connect the airport to the city center, ensuring a cost-effective commute.
Oulu Airport (OUL) - Northern Ostrobothnia	Nestled approximately 15 kilometers southwest of Oulu city center, Oulu Airport serves as a primary gateway to Northern Ostrobothnia.	Taxis, rental cars, and convenient bus services offer reliable transportation from the airport to Oulu and the surrounding areas.
Rovaniemi Airport (RVN) - Lapland	Located around 10 kilometers north of Rovaniemi city center, Rovaniemi Airport is the main gateway to the enchanting Lapland region.	Taxis, rental cars, and shuttle services provide efficient links between the airport and Rovaniemi. Public transportation options include buses that cater to various destinations within Lapland.
Kuopio Airport (KUO) - Northern Savonia	Approximately 14 kilometers northeast of Kuopio city center, Kuopio Airport serves as a key hub for Northern Savonia.	Taxis, car rentals, and convenient bus services connect the airport to Kuopio and neighboring areas. The well-maintained road infrastructure ensures smooth accessibility.

Vaasa Airport (VAA) - Ostrobothnia	About 9 kilometers southeast of Vaasa city center, Vaasa Airport is a prominent gateway to the Ostrobothnia region.	Taxis and rental cars are readily available, offering a swift journey to Vaasa and nearby areas. Buses also provide a cost-effective option, connecting the airport to various destinations.
Lappeenranta Airport (LPP) - Southeast Finland	Lappeenranta Airport is situated around 2.5 kilometers west of Lappeenranta city center, serving Southeast Finland.	Taxis, rental cars, and local bus services offer convenient transportation from the airport to Lappeenranta and the surrounding region. The proximity ensures quick and easy access to the city center.

Chapter 3: Helsinki and Its Regions

This chapter is devoted to Helsinki, the capital city of Finland. It will be your guide to learning all about the city's essential attractions and cultural experiences and includes practical travel tips. You will also gain insights into the city's history, iconic landmarks, famous cuisine, and shopping centers. It will even cover the various accommodation options (and the city's public transport system) and offers a glimpse into the city's entertainment options.

Helsinki, Finland.[8]

Did You Know?

Helsinki is known for its extensive and efficient public transportation system. It consists of a comprehensive underground network of tunnels and passageways called the "Keskuspuisto metro station." This station is not for trains but serves as a massive underground bus terminal that connects various bus lines and provides a convenient way for passengers to transfer between buses without having to go above ground.

Helsinki's History

Helsinki is Finland's capital, has a rich history, and is the largest and most populous city in the country. It was founded in 1550 by King Gustav I of Sweden. It became a trading hub due to its strategic location on the Gulf of Finland. A little-known fact outside the country is that Helsinki was wholly rebuilt in 1812 following a devastating fire in 1808. It was modeled on the architectural ideals of Russia's capital city, St Petersburg. It consists of neoclassical brick buildings and wide streets. The buildings in the city are made from light-colored granite stone, which is why it is called the white city of the North.

Toward the end of the 19th century, a railway system was built, the city was industrialized, and the inner-city tramline was brought into operation. Helsinki is located on the shores of the Baltic Sea. Its neighboring cities are Vantaa, Kauniainen, and Espoo, which make up the capital region. The city is also quite politically significant. It consists of the parliament house and the presidential palace. Moreover, it has also hosted a ton of international conferences, such as the Conference on Security and Cooperation in Europe in 1975. The city is also a vibrant cultural center with numerous theaters, museums, and galleries.

Attractions and Iconic Landmarks

Helsinki is rich in culture, history, and natural beauty. It has something to offer to everyone, regardless of whether you're looking to enjoy the outdoors, looking to try a delicious local cuisine, or exploring museums and theaters. Here are some great tourist spots to visit that can make your trip to this wonderful city one to remember.

Helsinki Cathedral

Helsinki Cathedral is one of the most iconic landmarks in Finland. It was built and designed in the 19th century by Carl Ludvig Engel. This neoclassical design symbolizes Finnish national identity. The church is admired for its outstanding architecture and the panoramic views of the city from the steps. It is a well-known Lutheran church, and it is also a symbol of Helsinki's religious and historical heritage.

As of the writing of this book, the opening hours are Sunday to Thursday from 9 am to 5 pm, Friday from 9 am to 2 pm, and closed on Saturday, However, please make sure to double-check the opening hours online should there be any changes to their schedule.

Address: Unioninkatu 29, 00170 Helsinki

Helsinki Cathedral.[9]

Senate Square

The Senate Square is surrounded by some of the most significant buildings, like the University of Helsinki, the Government Palace, and the National Library. This square was also designed by Carl Ludwig Engel and is used as a gathering place for events and festivals. The statue of Tsar Alexander II stands erect in the center of the square to commemorate his role in making Helsinki into the capital it is today.

As of the writing of this book, you can visit Senate Square any day at any time during your trip. However, please make sure to double-check the opening hours online should there be any changes to the schedule.

Address:00170 Helsinki

Senate Square.[10]

Suomenlinna Sea Fortress

Suomenlinna Sea Fortress is a UNESCO World Heritage Site. It is an island that was built in the 18th century to defend against naval threats. It has a long military and maritime history connected to Finland, Sweden, and Russia. Suomenlinna consists of well-preserved fortifications, museums, and tunnels to showcase the region's history. People also enjoy having picnics here as it offers a blend of both natural beauty and history.

As of the writing of this book, you can visit Senate Square any day at any time during your trip. However, please make sure to double-check the opening hours online should there be any changes to the schedule.

Address:00190 Helsinki

Suomenlinna Sea Fortress.[11]

Temppeliaukio Church (Rock Church)

Temppeliaukio Church is quite an interesting sight. It is carved into solid rock. The church is known for its exceptional acoustics and unique design and was completed in 1969. Many concerts and events are held in the Rock church, and it symbolizes Helinski's openness to modern architecture.

As of the writing of this book, the opening hours are as follows:

- Monday to Wednesday and Friday from 10 am to 4:50 pm.
- Thursday from 10 am to 4:35 pm.
- Saturday from 10 am to 11:35 am, 12:45 to 2:35 pm, 3:45 to 4:05 pm.
- Sunday from 12 pm to 4:50 pm.

However, please make sure to double-check the opening hours online should there be any slight changes to their schedule.

Address: Lutherinkatu 3, 00100 Helsinki

Temppeliaukio Church.[12]

Helsinki's Rich Cultural Scene

Helsinki has a wonderful cultural scene, and it truly reflects the country's rich history and contemporary creative expression. It is famous for its museums, theaters, music venues, and infamous design district.

Ateneum Art Museum

Ateneum Art Museum hosts artworks by well-known artists like Akseli Gallen-Kallela and Helene Schjerfbeck. It displays artworks from as early as the 18th century to the modern day. It is Finland's National Gallery and is truly worth visiting if you are an art enthusiast and want to understand the country's creative legacy.

As of the writing of this book, the opening hours are Tuesday to Friday from 10 am to 8 pm, Saturday and Sunday from 10 am to 5 pm, and closed on Monday. However, please make sure to double-check the opening hours online should there be any slight changes to their schedule.

Address: Kaivokatu 2, 00100 Helsinki

Ateneum Art Museum.[13]

Kiasma Museum of Contemporary Art

Kiasma Museum is also a part of the Finnish National Gallery and boasts contemporary artworks by modern artists. It has played an essential role in promoting young international and Finnish artists through its dynamic and diverse range of exhibitions.

As of the writing of this book, the opening hours are Tuesday to Friday from 10 am to 8 pm, Saturday and Sunday from 10 am to 5 pm, and closed on Monday. However, please make sure to double-check the opening hours online should there be any slight changes to their schedule.

Address: Mannerheiminaukio 2, 00100 Helsinki

Kiasma Museum.[14]

National Theatre

The National Theatre was founded in 1872 and is one of the oldest Finnish-language professional theaters in the country. It has a strong history of creating classic and modern Finnish plays that have significantly contributed to the development of Finnish theater arts.

As of the writing of this book, the opening hours are Monday to Friday from 10 am to 5 pm (10 am to 7 pm on performance days, Saturday from 11 am to 7 pm, and closed on Sunday. However, please make sure to double-check the opening hours online should there be any slight changes to their schedule.

Address: Lantinen Teatterikuja 1, 00100 Helsinki

The National Theatre.[15]

Music Venues

If you have an affinity for live music and gigs, then Helsinki has a lot to offer the musically minded. It is a hub for music enthusiasts with numerous musical venues that cater to all tastes. The city is also well known for hosting concerts ranging from contemporary to classical music. Some of the iconic venues include Finlandia Hall, Helsinki Music Centre, and the Tavastia Club. Each one offers a unique musical experience.

As of the writing of this book the opening hours for Finlandia Hall are Monday to Friday from 9 am to 9 pm, and Saturday and Sunday from 11 am to 9 pm. The opening hours for the Helsinki Music Centre are Monday to Friday from 8 am to 10 pm, and Saturday and Sunday from 10 am to 8 pm. The opening hours for Tavastia Club depend on the shows available. However, please make sure to double-check the opening hours online should there be any slight changes to their schedule.

Finlandia Hall Address: Mannerheimintie 13 E, 00100 Helsinki

Helsinki Music Centre Address: Mannerheimintie 13 A, 00100 Helsinki

Tavastia Club Address: Urho Kekkosen katu 4, 00100 Helsinki

Helsinki Music Centre.[16]

Design District

If you are interested in Finnish design, then you must visit Helsinki's Design District. This district consists of several streets in the heart of the city and houses a cluster of galleries, boutiques, and studios that boast the best of Finnish design. Visitors are free to explore and buy high-quality Finnish products, ranging from furniture to jewelry. The Design Museum is worth visiting as it provides insights into the history of Finnish design and the Marimekko Flagship store, which is famous for its Finnish clothing designs and textiles.

As of the writing of this book, you can visit the Helsinki Design District at any time during your trip. The Design Museum is open Tuesday from 11 am to 8 pm, Wednesday to Sunday from 11 am to 6 pm, and is closed on Monday. The Marimekko Flagship store is open Tuesday, Wednesday, Friday and Monday from 10 am to 8 pm, Thursday from 10 am to 5:30 pm, Saturday from 10 am to 6 pm, and Sunday from 12 pm to 6 pm.

Helsinki Design District Address: Korkeavuorenkatu 7, 00140 Helsinki

Design Museum Address: Korkeavuorenkatu 23, 00130 Helsinki

Marimekko Flagship Store Address: Pohjoisesplanadi 33, 00100 Helsinki

The Design Museum.[17]

The Design District also hosts events like Helsinki Design Week to attract design professionals and enthusiasts from all over the world. Artists are able to showcase their designs, and the latest trends in design are celebrated during the festival. The Finnish design is celebrated for its simplicity, functionality, and timeless aesthetics. Many well-known designers like Eero Saarinen, Artek, and Alvar Aalto have made significant contributions to the global design arena.

Local Dining and Cuisine

Finnish cuisine is distinguished by its fresh and locally sourced ingredients. In the Baltic Sea countries, herring, salmon, pork, and goose are staples. They also hunt reindeer for food, and most meats are smoked and salted. Various eateries in Helsinki are waiting to offer you the experience of traditional Finnish dishes. Here are some recommendations for places where you can try classic Finnish delicacies.

Name	Information	Address
Savotta	Savotta offers genuine Finnish food and atmosphere. "Savotta" means a logging site. The interior design and the dishes themselves are inspired by the forests and lakes and the Finnish logging tradition. The menu consists of traditional Finnish dishes, including game meats and fish. It's a great place to try dishes like Karjalanpiirakka and Lohikeitto in a cozy atmosphere.	Aleksanterinkatu 22, 00170 Helsinki
Kappeli	Kappeli is one of the historic restaurants located in the heart of Helsinki known for its classic Finnish dishes. The menu consists of Lihapullat (Finnish meatballs) served with mashed potatoes and lingonberry sauce, which offers a taste of traditional Finnish comfort food.	Eteläesplanadi 1, 00130 Helsinki
Sea Horse	The Sea Horse restaurant was established in 1934 and is one	Kapteeninkatu 11,

	of the oldest restaurants in Helsinki. It offers a wide variety of menus that focus on Nordic and Finnish foods. Traditional dishes like Lohikeitto (Salmon Soup) and other seafood dishes are some of the specialties available here.	00140 Helsinki
Sipuli	Sipuli is situated in an old warehouse by the sea. It is known for its Finnish cuisine with a modern twist. The menu consists of traditional dishes which can be enjoyed with the beautiful scenery of the harbor.	Kanavaranta 7, 00160 Helsinki

Shopping Guide

Helsinki offers an outstanding shopping experience to tourists from all over the world with its exquisite shopping centers, traditional markets, and districts. Here are some renowned shopping destinations that you must visit to get the full experience:

Name	Information	Address
Kamppi Center	Kamppi Center is located in the city center and is one of the largest shopping centers in Helsinki. It consists of all sorts of boutiques, shops, cafes, and restaurants. You will easily find a plethora of international and Finnish brands, which makes it an attractive one-stop destination for all your shopping needs.	Urho Kekkosen katu 1, 00100 Helsinki

Forum Shopping Center	Another well-known shopping destination is the Forum Shopping Center. It houses a variety of stores, including electronics, fashion, and beauty. The mall is famous for its contemporary atmosphere and popular brands, which attract tourists and locals alike.	Mannerheimintie 14-20, 00100 Helsinki
Stockmann Department Store	Stockmann Department Store is not just a historic department store but also an iconic landmark in Helsinki. It was established in 1862 and offers a diverse range of products, from cosmetics to fashion to home appliances to gourmet food. Stockmann is famous for its high-quality selection and pleasant shopping experience.	Aleksanterinkatu 52, 00100 Helsinki
Design District	Design District, as mentioned above, is a must-visit for all art enthusiasts. It houses various streets in the city center, including Punavuori and Kallio. You will find all kinds of galleries, boutiques, and studios displaying the best Finnish design has to offer, including furniture, home decor, and clothing.	
Market Square	Market Square is a bright and traditional market located near	Eteläranta, 00170 Helsinki

(Kauppatori)	the sea. It is a great place to experience traditional Finish market culture. The market stalls exhibit a variety of goods, including fresh produce, souvenirs, and local crafts. The square hosts a popular Christmas market in winter.	

Accommodation Options

When it comes to accommodation, Helsinki has a wide variety of options for all types of travelers. Whether you're vacationing on a budget or are looking for luxury hotels, there is something for everyone. Here are some great recommendations that also hold cultural and historical value:

Hotel Kämp

The Hotel Kamp has been known as a symbol of elegance in Helsinki since 1887. It is a classical luxury hotel famous for hosting celebrities such as Whitney Houston, Madonna, and Bruce Springsteen. It is one of Finland's top five-star hotels. It offers suites with classical decor, modern facilities, and world-class service. It also has its very own restaurant, Brasserie Kämp, which serves French-inspired cuisine.

Address: Pohjoisesplanadi 29, 00100 Helsinki

Hotel Lilla Roberts

Hotel Lilla Roberts is a chic hotel located in a beautifully restored power plant building in the Design District. Its rooms are designed to offer optimal comfort with style to its guests. If you want to explore the creative scene in the city while staying in a comfortable location, then this would be an excellent place for you to stay.

Address: Pieni Roobertinkatu 1, 00130 Helsinki

Eurohostel

This is a great budget-friendly accommodation option for you if you're looking for a clean and practical option. You will be able to enjoy these comfortable rooms with shared facilities without compromising on convenience.

Address: Linnankatu 9, 00160 Helsinki

City's Public Transport System

Helinski has an excellent public transport system that mainly consists of buses and trams. Buses provide extensive coverage across the city and the surrounding areas. Trams are a more popular and convenient way of getting to the city center and exploring the surrounding neighborhood areas. It also has an excellent metro system, offering a fast and convenient mode of transportation by linking the city center to the eastern suburbs. If you are looking to visit the Helsinki Archipelago, then ferries are your best bet. The municipal ferry operated by HSL runs between Market Square and the Suomenlinna Sea Fortress all year round. The ferry terminal is located on the east side of Market Square, opposite the Presidential Palace.

You may want to consider getting a Helsinki Card or travel pass for unlimited access to public transport. These cards often come with wonderful perks like free entry to museums and discounts at various destinations. The city also has a great bike system that allows tourists to rent bikes for short trips. The city is quite bike-friendly, with dedicated bike lanes and flat topography. Various bike rental shops offer electric bikes as well for longer journeys. The city is also highly walkable, with many restaurants, shops, and major attractions at reasonable distances from each other.

If you are traveling by car, then the journey will be more convenient for you. Helsinki has parking garages and street parking. However, it can be challenging to find parking in the city center. There are parking apps as well that can help you find parking spaces and pay for them.

Day Trips and Tours from Helsinki

You can find many day trip opportunities in Helsinki. Here are some recommendations:

Nuuksio National Park

Nuuksio National Park is known for its forests, lakes, and rocky landscapes. You can go for guided nature walks, and wildlife spotting, and even book a Finnish sauna experience. There are companies like Nuuksio Classic that offer you guided tours including hiking and canoeing experiences.

Distance from Helsinki: Approximately 40 km northwest of Helsinki.

Address: Nuuksiontie 84, 02820 Espoo

Porvoo

Porvoo is famous for its well-preserved medieval old town. You can walk along cobblestone streets, hang out in the famous red-painted warehouses, and explore local boutiques. Many tour companies like the Porvoo Tours offer guided day trips and also provide historical knowledge and insights. They also offer you free time to explore the place on your own.

Distance from Helsinki: About 50 km east of Helsinki.

Archipelago Cruise

You can visit the numerous beautiful islands scattered along the coast by getting on a picturesque archipelago cruise. You can visit the local villages, enjoy the calmness of the sea, and savor the unique island culture. There are companies like Redrib Experience that offer guided excursions with great options for island visits and lunch. (https://redrib.fi/en/)

Distance from Helsinki: Various islands in the Helsinki Archipelago.

Family-Friendly Options

There are various family-friendly options available to explore as well. Here are some of the places you can explore:

Linnanmäki Amusement Park

Linnanmäki is a well-known amusement park in Helsinki offering a wide range of entertainment options for visitors of all ages, including rides and games. It has something for everyone, from fun-filled days out with thrilling options like roller coasters to family-friendly attractions. It also hosts live shows and has a carnival area with snacks and games.

Location: Tivoli Kuja 1, 00510 Helsinki

Helsinki Zoo on Korkeasaari Island

If you're looking to have great interactive fun with your family – the Helsinki Zoo (on Korkeasaari Island) is a fantastic destination! It houses a great variety of animals from all over the world, and it also has themed exhibits like the Amazonian rainforest.

Location: Mustikkamaanpolku 12, 00570 Helsinki

Heureka, the Finnish Science Centre

Heureka is a wonderful interactive science center situated outside Helsinki in Vantaa. It provides you with activities designed to engage and educate visitors about science and technology. It gives families a chance to explore different thematic zones, partake in workshops, and enjoy educational shows, which makes it a wonderful place to explore for budding scientists and curious minds.

Location: Tiedepuisto 1, 01300 Vantaa

Natural History Museum

The Natural History Museum in Helsinki is a great educational and engaging destination for families. It boasts interactive displays and educational programs that cater to both children and adults. It also displays exhibits showing the diversity of life on Earth, such as minerals, fossils, and stuffed animals.

Location: Pohjoinen Rautatiekatu 13, 00100 Helsinki

Entertainment, Nightlife, and Festivals

Throughout the year, Helsinki hosts many events that celebrate its culture, history, and community. Helsinki has a vibrant atmosphere that ensures a great and memorable experience for everyone. With its lively festivals, live music scene, and amazing nightlife, Helsinki is an unforgettable experience.

Helsinki Day (Helsingin päivä)

Helsinki Day celebrates the city's birthday with a wide range of events, such as cultural performances, concerts, and other activities taking place all over the city. The tourists and locals come together to celebrate the wonderful community spirit of Helsinki.

Date: June 12th

Vappu (May Day)

Vappu marks the arrival of spring. This event is celebrated with picnics, concerts, and traditional student gatherings. People wear white student caps and fill the streets to enjoy the cheerful atmosphere.

Date: May 1st

Helsinki Festival

The Helsinki Festival is an annual multidisciplinary arts festival that features a wide variety of cultural events like dance, music, visual arts, theater, and more. The festival takes place at different venues across the city, boasting international and Finnish artists alike. Do look for local information, as dates and locations vary from year to year.

Date: The last two weeks of August

Korjaamo

Korjaamo is known for hosting various concerts, theater performances, art exhibitions, and club nights. It is a cultural venue situated in a former tram depot. The venue has an industrial-chic atmosphere that adds to its unique charm.

Location: Töölönkatu 51 a-b, 00250 Helsinki

Gloria

Gloria is an infamous live music venue in Helsinki that hosts many performances like concerts, club nights, and cultural events. It features a diverse lineup of artists and is known for its immaculate vibe.

Location: Pieni Roobertinkatu 12, 00120 Helsinki

Kulttuurisauna

Kulttuurisauna is a one-of-a-kind cultural venue and public sauna situated by the sea. It hosts wonderful cultural events, performances, and exhibitions in addition to offering a traditional sauna experience.

Location: Hakaniemenranta 17, 00530 Helsinki

All in all, if you are looking for a place that will offer you the best of both worlds in terms of historical significance and modernity, Helsinki is the place for you. You will find something to match your interests in the city, from scenic islands to modern art exhibitions. This chapter explored various accommodation options and transport systems in detail. It also discussed various entertainment options for families and individuals alike. In short, Helsinki will undoubtedly offer an unforgettable experience that you will always cherish.

Chapter 4: Uusimaa and Southwest Finland

Brief Historical Background

Uusimaa is a region in southern Finland, and within it lies the city of Espoo, which is the second-largest city in the country. Espoo is recognized as a thriving innovation hub, hosting prominent research and educational institutions like the VTT Technical Research Centre and Aalto University. The city is also home to major global corporations such as Nokia, and Kone. Notably, all of Finland's unicorns, including successful game companies like Rovio originated in Espoo. (A unicorn company is a privately owned one that achieved a valuation of over $1 billion.)

Uusimaa.[18]

Vantaa, another city in southern Finland, is one of the most populous cities in the region, with over 247,443 inhabitants. It is renowned for hosting one of Finland's busiest airports, the Helsinki-Vantaa Airport, acting as a significant international gateway. Beyond its aviation prominence, Vantaa offers a mix of historic and modern attractions, making it an ideal destination for families, especially those with aviation enthusiasts.

Kauniainen, with approximately 10,270 inhabitants, is a cozy modern suburb situated within the municipality of Espoo. Known for its tranquility and natural beauty, this city is a perfect getaway from urban hustle and bustle. With a blend of Finnish and Swedish speakers, Kauniainen offers lush green areas, parks, and gardens for visitors to explore and enjoy a peaceful atmosphere.

Porvoo, located on the southern coast of Finland, stands out as one of the country's oldest and most charming cities. Recognized for its well-preserved houses, rich marine history, and iconic red warehouses along the river, Porvoo offers a unique blend of romantic ambiance and historical significance.

Kirkkonummi, also in southern Finland, attracts visitors with its enchanting mix of natural beauty and historical importance. The town is known for its picturesque landscapes, making it an appealing destination for various tourists.

Salo, situated in southwestern Finland, gained prominence due to its connection with Nokia. Although Nokia's influence has evolved, Salo still draws tech enthusiasts and tourists from around the world. The city is celebrated for its tech legacy and serene countryside.

Naantali.[19]

Naantali is a popular summer city in Finland, offering a diverse range of attractions for visitors. With a combination of family-friendly destinations, historical landmarks, and relaxing experiences, Naantali captures the essence of a perfect summer retreat.

Did You Know?

Did you know that Uusimaa and Southwest Finland are home to the Archipelago Sea, which is the largest archipelago in the world by number of islands? The Archipelago Sea consists of thousands of islands and skerries that create a stunning and unique maritime landscape. It is not only a beautiful natural attraction but also a popular destination for boating, island hopping, and enjoying the serene coastal environment.

Attractions and Iconic Landmarks

Archipelago

Espoo has a wealth of natural landscapes worth visiting. The city has 58 kilometers of shoreline in the municipality and has much to offer tourists who have an affinity for the sea. There are around 165 islands in the archipelago that can be explored by tourists who have a love for boating and fishing.

Nuuksio National Park

In the North of Espoo lies the Nuuksio National Park, which consists of beautiful forests and lakes. The park is just a short distance from the city center. You will be able to tour picturesque lakes, rocky landscapes, and lush forests, which makes it an excellent place for wildlife spotting, hiking, and reconnecting with nature. The national park offers wonderful opportunities for locals and tourists alike to embrace the outdoors and rejuvenate.

As of the writing of this book, you can visit Nuuksio National Park at any time on any day during your trip. However, please make sure to double-check the opening hours online should there be any slight changes to their schedule.

Address: Nuuksiontie 84, 02820 Espoo

Nuuksio National Park.[20]

Espoo Museum of Modern Art (EMMA)

Espoo Museum of Modern Art (EMMA) is an embodiment of artistic expression. Found in the WeeGee building, EMMA showcases a comprehensive collection of contemporary and classic art pieces by Finnish and international artists. The WeeGee building itself is an architectural wonder that adds to the cultural allure of the museum. EMMA is a treat for all art lovers as it blends both innovation and creativity.

As of the writing of this book, the opening hours for the Espoo Museum of Modern Art are Tuesday, Saturday, and Sunday from 11 am to 5 pm, Wednesday and Thursday from 11 am to 7 pm, Friday from 11 am to 9 pm, and is closed on Monday. However, please make sure to double-check the opening hours online should there be any slight changes to their schedule.

Address: Ahertajantie 5, 02070 Espoo

EMMA.[21]

Aviation Museum Society

The Aviation Museum Society was founded by a group of volunteers and aviation enthusiasts in 1969 with the goal of eventually creating a Finnish Aviation Museum to preserve aviation history. The museum was finally opened in the heart of the Aviapolis area in Vantaa in 1981. It boasts a remarkable collection of aircraft and aviation-related artifacts. It offers a rich experience for those fascinated by the history of both military and civil aviation.

As of the writing of this book, the opening hours for the Finnish Aviation Museum are Tuesday, Saturday, and Sunday from 10 am to 5 pm, Wednesday to Friday from 10 am to 8 pm, and is closed on Monday. However, please make sure to double-check the opening hours online should there be any slight changes to their schedule.

Address: Karhumaentie 12, 01530 Vantaa

Heureka, the Finnish Science Centre

Heureka, the Finnish Science Centre, is another wonderful place that is a must-visit. This science center offers a great educational and interactive experience to visitors of all ages. It offers hands-on activities and engaging exhibits that are sure to make anyone fall in love with science. Heureka's goal is to ensure that science and technology are easily accessible and enjoyed by everyone.

As of the writing of this book, the opening hours for are Monday to Wednesday and Friday from 10 am to 5 pm, Thursday from 10 am to 8 pm, Saturday and Sunday from 10 am to 6 pm, and is closed on Monday. However, please make sure to double-check the opening hours online should there be any slight changes to their schedule.

Address: Tiedepuisto 1, 01300 Vantaa

Heureka.[22]

Church of St. Lawrence

The 15th-century Church of St. Lawrence is a historical landmark in Vantaa. This medieval church boasts stunning architecture that offers a glimpse into the city's rich religious and cultural heritage.

As of the writing of this book, the opening hours are Tuesday, Thursday and Friday from 12 pm to 3 pm, and is closed on Wednesday and Saturday to Monday. However, please make sure to double-check the opening hours online should there be any slight changes to their schedule.

Address: Kirkkotie 45, 01510 Vantaa

Church of St. Lawrence.[23]

Residential Community of Kauniainen

Kauniainen is majorly a residential area with a close-knit community that offers a more authentic experience to tourists who are looking for a more local and intimate setting. Moreover, it also hosts cultural and community events to display local talent and harbor a sense of community. These small events allow the locals and visitors a chance to experience the city's uniqueness firsthand and connect with locals.

Porvoo's Old Town

Porvoo's Old Town is a scenic area with cobblestone streets and well-preserved wooden houses painted in vibrant colors. Walking among these charming streets takes you back in time and gives you a glimpse of the city's medieval past.

As of the writing of this book, you can visit Porvoo's Old Town at any time during your trip. However, please make sure to double-check the opening hours online should there be any slight changes to their schedule.

Address: 06100 Porvoo

Porvoo's Old Town.[24]

The Porvoo Cathedral

The Porvoo Cathedral is another site you won't want to miss! It was built in the 15th century and is an important architectural masterpiece of the medieval era. Its red-brick facade adds to the visual appeal of the city. The interior consists of beautiful artworks and historical artifacts.

As of the writing of this book, the opening hours are Monday to Friday from 10 am to 6 pm, Saturday from 10 am to 2 pm, and Sunday from 2 pm to 5 pm. However, please make sure to double-check the opening hours online should there be any slight changes to their schedule.

Address: Kirkkotori 1, 06100 Porvoo

The Porvoo Cathedral.[25]

The Porvoo Museum

The Porvoo Museum offers a deep insight into the city's history. It is located inside charming buildings and exhibits displays related to Porvoo's past, including the marine heritage, evolution of Porvoo's culture, and the lives of its people throughout different eras.

As of the writing of this book, the opening hours are Wednesday from 12 pm to 6 pm, Thursday to Sunday from 12 pm to 4 pm, and is closed on Monday and Tuesday. However, please make sure to double-check the opening hours online should there be any slight changes to their schedule.

Address: Valikatu 11, 06100 Porvoo

The Porvoo Museum.[26]

Porvoo's romantic charm

Porvoo's romantic charm is reflected by its intimate restaurants, cafés, and unique boutiques. It's an excellent place for couples to enjoy strolls through the Old Town while exploring the local shops offering handmade goodies and antiques. Porvoo also boasts a wide range of culinary expertise with a range of international and local cuisines. The great culinary experience offered makes it an ideal destination for couples. Overall, the city has much to offer to history buffs, families, and couples.

Kirkkonummi Church

The medieval stone church in the town center stands as a witness to the town's resilient past. The church boasts timeless architecture and holds great religious and cultural value. It also invites visitors to explore its interior and connect to the rich heritage of Kirkkonummi.

As of the writing of this book, you need to book a session online to enter the church depending on your purpose, but you can stroll around the premises at any time. However, please make sure to double-check when you can visit the church online should there be any changes.

Address: Tallinmaki 1, 02400 Kirkkonummi

Kirkkonummi Church.[27]

The Hvitträsk Museum

In addition to the church, Kirkkonummi has many other historical sites and landmarks that add to the beauty and depth of the town. Exploring these places will give you a better sense of the city's evolution over the years. The Hvitträsk Museum lies at a short distance from Kirkkonummi. Built in the early 20th century, the museum is a cultural gem that offers great historical and architectural significance. The museum was the home of renowned Finnish architects, including Eliel Saarinen. It offers a sneak peek into the lives and creative motivations of these influential people.

As of the writing of this book, the opening hours are Wednesday to Sunday from 11 am to 5 pm, and is closed on Monday and Tuesday. However, please make sure to double-check the opening hours online should there be any slight changes to their schedule.

Address: Hvittraskintie 166, 02440 Kirkkonummi

The Hvitträsk Museum.[28]

Pampskatan Outdoor Area in Kirkkonummi

If you're a nature lover, then you would undoubtedly appreciate Kirkkonummi's natural beauty that can be witnessed through its extensive coastline, beautiful lakes, and lush green forests. You can immerse yourself in the tranquility of nature and explore the diverse flora and fauna of the region. You can also go for a hike or birdwatch with your family. There are water-based activities available as well in Kirkkonummi.

The Loviisa Fortress

Loviisa is a pleasant little seaside town in southern Finland that welcomes visitors with its setting, historical landmarks, and peaceful coastal ambiance. The Loviisa Fortress is a well-known historical landmark that attracts history fanatics and curious travelers alike. This fortress offers a glimpse into the city's strategic importance. Tourists can explore the fortress grounds and learn about the town's role in the history of Finland.

As of the writing of this book, you can visit the Loviisa Fortress at any time during your trip. However, please make sure to double-check the opening hours online should there be any slight changes to their schedule.

Address: Kuhlefeltinkatu, 07900 Loviisa

Loviisa.[29]

Loviisa's Old Town

Loviisa's Old Town consists of cobblestone streets and rich architectural heritage. Walking through the streets is like taking a trip back in time. Loviisa's harbor is a site to be seen. Its picturesque environment offers a peaceful escape from the hustle of the city. Visitors can experience the scenic view on a gentle boat ride. The harbor is a great place to sit, relax, and take in the sea breeze.

As of the writing of this book, you can visit Loviisa's Old Town at any time during your trip. However, please make sure to double-check the opening hours online should there be any slight changes to their schedule.

Address: Brandensteininkatu, 07900 Loviisa.

Loviisa's café and local shops add to the beauty of the town. The little cafés along the streets create a cozy environment for enjoying local delicacies and beverages.

Sipoonkorpi National Park

From dense forests to open fields, visitors to this park have a lot to explore. The changing scenery will be very refreshing! Outdoor fanatics will especially appreciate the Sipoonkorpi National Park as it is a haven for hiking and nature exploration. The park has well-marked trails through the beautiful forests, displaying the beauty of the region. It is the ideal destination for those who want to seek peace and connect to Finland's wilderness.

As of the writing of this book, you can visit Sipoonkorpi National Park at any time during your trip. However, please make sure to double-check the opening hours online should there be any slight changes to their schedule.

Address: 04130 Sipoo

Sipoonkorpi National Park.[30]

Sipoo's Waterfronts

Sipoo's waterfronts, whether it is the archipelago or the lakes, offer a calming and tranquil setting. You can take long walks along the shore to enjoy the calming influence of the waterfront ambiance. Sipoo's archipelago is a prize in itself. You can go island hopping and boating – discovering the islands; all of them are brimming with activities that add to their allure!

The Sipoo Old Church

The Sipoo Old Church is a historical landmark built entirely out of wood. This architectural gem was built in the 17th century and adds to the city's mystique. It offers excellent insight into the cultural and religious history of the town.

As of the writing of this book, the Sipoo Old Church is open daily during the summer for visits. However, please make sure to double-check the opening hours online should there be any slight changes to their schedule.

Address: Brobolentie 68, 04130 Sipoo

The Sipoo Old Church.[31]

Teijo National Park

The city offers many opportunities for people to explore nature and its picturesque countryside, particularly in Teijo National Park. You can engage in numerous outdoor activities at the park, including going on hiking trails through the forests and enjoying the scenic lakes.

As of the writing of this book, you can visit Teijo National Park at any time during your trip. However, please make sure to double-check the opening hours online should there be any slight changes to their schedule.

Address: Matildanjarventie 84, 25660 Salo

Mathildedal Ironworks Village

If you're looking for insight into the local industrial history, then there's no better place to learn about it than the cultural hub that is the Mathildedal Ironworks Village. You can explore the ironwork building while gaining an understanding of the region's past. There are charming cafés and shops as well that add to the village's aesthetic.

As of the writing of this book, you can visit Mathildedal Ironworks Village at any time during your trip. However, please make sure to double-check the opening hours online should there be any slight changes to their schedule.

Address: Ruukinrannantie 6, 25660 Salo

The Moomin World Theme Park

The Moomin World Theme Park is a major attraction for families as it has something to offer to everyone. The theme park is based on the Moomin characters created by Tove Jansson, the Finnish author. The park's enchanting and engaging atmosphere makes it a must-visit destination for families with children to help their imaginations go wild.

As of the writing of this book, the opening hours are from 11 am to 5 pm during June and August, and from 10 am to 5 pm during July. The hours are subject to change during the winter months. However, please make sure to double-check the opening hours online should there be any slight changes to their schedule.

Address: Kaivokatu 5, 21101 Naantali

Naantali's Old Town

Naantali's Old Town is a charming little area with traditional wooden houses, cobblestone streets, and a picturesque atmosphere. You can take long strolls in the street while appreciating the beautifully well-preserved houses in the coastal town.

As of the writing of this book, you can visit Naantali's Old Town at any time during your trip. However, please make sure to double-check the opening hours online should there be any slight changes to their schedule.

Address: Vanhakaipunki, 21100 Naantali

Naantali's Old Town [32].

The Naantali Convent Church

The Naantali Convent Church dates back to the medieval era and is known as the historical landmark in Naantali. Its medieval architecture and calm environment contribute to the town's cultural heritage.

As of the writing of this book, the opening hours are Tuesday to Sunday from 11 am to 6 pm and is closed on Monday. However, please make sure to double-check the opening hours online should there be any slight changes to their schedule.

Address: Nunnakatu 2, 21100 Naantali

The Naantali Convent Church. [33]

Naantali Spa

Another interesting thing about Naantali is that one of the largest spas in the Nordic countries is found there. You can unwind and indulge yourself in spa treatments and saunas and make use of therapeutic amenities to make yourself fully relaxed. This will make Naantali an ideal destination if you are looking for a rejuvenating experience.

As of the writing of this book, the Naantali Spa is open 24 hours. However, please make sure to double-check the opening hours online should there be any slight changes to their schedule.

Address: Matkailijantie 2, 21100 Naantali

Naantali Guest Harbor

The guest harbor in Naantali adds to the overall vibrant feel of the cityscape. The cafés, shops, and the different-sized boats along the waterfront create a unique atmosphere. Naantali Guest Harbor is the perfect place to indulge in the maritime ambiance while enjoying the archipelago. The allure of Naanrali as a leisure destination is improved by its seaside location and cultural significance, and it gives you time to relax in a beautiful setting. Naantali has something to offer to all its visitors.

As of the writing of this book, you can visit Naantali Guest Harbor at any time during your trip. However, please make sure to double-check the opening hours online should there be any slight changes to their schedule.

Address: Nunnakatu 18, 21100 Naantali

The Bonk Museum

The Bonk Museum is a witness to Uusikaupunki's industrial past and its nautical heritage. Visitors can explore the museum's exhibits to learn more about the city's maritime history, including the seafaring traditions and shipbuilding. The museum also offers insights into the Uusikaupunki's significance in Finland's naval history.

As of the writing of this book, the opening hours are Tuesday to Saturday from 11 am to 3 pm from the 4th of June to the 20th of June and from the 10th of August to the 25th of August, and every day from 10 am to 6 pm from the 24th of June to the 6th of August. Hours for the rest of the year have not yet been stated. However, please make sure to double-check the opening hours online should there be any slight changes to their schedule.

Address: Siltakatu 2, 23500 Uusikaupunki

Automuseum

Uusikaupunki's industrial legacy in the field of automobile manufacturing is vividly celebrated by the Automuseum. The museum showcases an extensive collection of historic cars and offers a journey through the evolution of automotive engineering in Finland.

As of the writing of this book, the opening hours are every day from 11 am to 5 pm. However, please make sure to double-check the opening hours online should there be any slight changes to their schedule.

Address: Autotehtaankatu 11, 23500 Uusikaupunki

Pakkahuone Guest Harbor

Pakkahuone Guest Harbor has boats of all sizes, waterfront cafés, and cozy little shops. The scenic views make this place a great spot to relax and unwind.

As of the writing of this book, you can visit at any time during your trip. The cafes are open from 8 am to 8 pm. However, please make sure to double-check the opening hours online should there be any slight changes to their schedule.

Address: Pakkahuoneetoru 2, Kaupunginlahti, Uusikaupunki

Isokari Lighthouse Island

Another must-see destination in Uusikaupunki is the Isokari Lighthouse Island. The island has a historic lighthouse that offers a breathtaking view of the surrounding archipelago.

As of the writing of this book, you can visit the Isokari Lighthouse Island at any time during your trip. However, please make sure to double-check the opening hours online should there be any slight changes to their schedule.

Address: Isokari, 23500 Uusikaupunki

Where to Eat in Uusimaa and Southwest Finland

Name	Information	Address
GLO Hotel Sello (Espoo)	Located in the heart of Leppävaara, this stylish hotel offers a restaurant with a diverse menu, blending Finnish and international flavors.	Leppavaarankatu 1, 02600 Espoo
Restaurant Nokkalen Majakka (Espoo)	Situated near the shores of the Gulf of Finland, this restaurant focuses on using locally sourced, high-quality ingredients to create traditional Finnish dishes.	Nokkalanniemi 2, 02230 Espoo
Ravintola La Locanda (Vantaa)	This restaurant offers a variety of cuisines, including Turkish, Italian, and Middle Eastern.	Maitikkakuja 1, 01350 Vantaa
Bistro Liekki (Vantaa)	This bistro serves a variety of dishes, including smash burgers, grills, and traditional Finnish dishes.	Talvikkitie 30, 01300 Vantaa
Chalipa Food Machete	This cozy restaurant in Kauniainen offers a	Tunnelitie 1, 02700

(Kauniainen)	relaxed atmosphere and a menu featuring Mexican dishes.	Kauniainen
Lahella Deli (Kauniainen)	Perfect for a leisurely afternoon, this deli is known for its pastries and sandwiches, providing a peaceful break from exploring the green areas.	Torin laidalla, Thurmanunaukio 10, 02700 Kauniainen
Porvoon Paahtimo Bar & Café (Porvoo)	The great culinary experience offered by the Porvoon Paahtimo Bar & Café makes it an ideal destination for couples.	Mannerheiminkatu 2, 06100 Porvoo
SicaPelle (Porvoo)	Situated in the heart of Porvoo's Old Town, this restaurant offers a blend of Italian and Nordic cuisine in a historic setting.	Kirkkotori 3, 06100 Porvoo
Hanna-Maria (Porvoo)	Known for its traditional Finnish dishes, Hanna-Maria is a cozy restaurant with a welcoming atmosphere.	Valikatu 6, 06100 Porvoo
La Gabbana (Kirkkonummi)	This restaurant offers a blend of international cuisines to suit everyone's taste,	Asemankaari, 02400 Kirkkonummi

	including Italian, American, and Middle Eastern cuisines.	
Hanami Sushi (Kirkkonummi)	A classy restaurant in Kirkkonummi serving sushi and Japanese cuisine.	Kirkkotallintie 2 A 2, 02400 Kirkkonummi
Kappeli Loviisa (Loviisa)	Set in a historic building, this restaurant offers a diverse menu with a focus on local ingredients, providing a taste of traditional Finnish cuisine.	Kuningatterenkatu 19, 07900 Loviisa
Favorit Café and Tea (Loviisa)	A cozy café in Loviisa, known for its coffee, homemade pastries and wonderful atmosphere.	Aleksanterinkatu 6, 07900 Loviisa
Ravintola Tila (Sipoo)	This restaurant offers delicious dishes made with high-quality ingredients.	Knutersintie 262, 04130 Sipoo
Restaurant PortSide Trattoria (Sipoo)	A restaurant situated near the water and serves Italian cuisine. Enjoy your meal with a wonderful view.	Sipoonranta 10, 01120 Sipoo
Wanha Mestari (Salo)	This restaurant in Salo combines Finnish and European cuisine in a	Turuntie 2, 24100 Salo

	relaxed atmosphere, perfect for a casual meal.	
Café Mathildedal (Matilda)	A charming café in Mathildedal Ironworks Village, known for its pastries and coffee, providing a delightful break during exploration.	Ruukinrannantie 8, 25660 Matilda
Mamma's Kitchen (Naantali)	Inside the Moomin World theme park, this snack bar offers family-friendly meals with a Moomin-inspired touch.	Kailo Muumimaailmaa, 21100 Naantali
Hasta la Pasta (Naantali)	Near the guest harbor, this restaurant provides delicious pasta dishes and desserts.	Alikatu 9, 21100 Naantali
Ravintola Captain's Makasiini (Uusikaupunki)	Located near the Pakkahuoneenranta guest harbor, this seafood restaurant offers a taste of the region's maritime flavors.	Aittaranta 12, 23500 Uusikaupunki

Transportation in Uusimaa and Southwest Finland

Uusimaa, including southwest Finland, has a well-developed transportation infrastructure that includes various options for getting around the region. Here are some of the transportation options you can find:

Public Transportation

Trains: The Finnish railway network connects many cities in Uusimaa, offering efficient and comfortable train services. Helsinki Central Railway Station is a major hub.

Buses: Public buses operate extensively, providing connectivity to both urban and rural areas. Helsinki Region Transport (HSL) manages public transportation in the Helsinki metropolitan area.

Metro: Helsinki has a metro system that serves the city and extends to neighboring Espoo.

Air Travel

Helsinki-Vantaa Airport: Located in Vantaa, this is the main international airport serving the region. It is a significant hub for both domestic and international flights.

Cars: The road network in Uusimaa is well-maintained, and driving is a common mode of transportation. Highways and roads connect all the major cities and towns.

Taxis: Taxis are readily available in urban areas and can be hailed on the street or booked in advance.

Bike Paths: Many cities in Uusimaa, especially Helsinki and Espoo, have dedicated bike paths, making cycling a popular and eco-friendly mode of transportation.

Ferries

Ferry Services: Due to the coastal nature of the region, ferry services operate between islands and coastal areas. Naantali, for example, may have ferry connections to suit your holiday requirements.

Car Rentals

Rental Services: Car rental services are available for those who prefer the flexibility of driving themselves.

Pedestrian-Friendly Areas: Many urban centers, especially those in Helsinki, are designed to be pedestrian-friendly with well-maintained sidewalks and pedestrian zones.

Regional Rail Services

Commuter Trains: Commuter trains connect various towns and suburbs in the Uusimaa region, facilitating daily commuting for residents.

Shopping Guide

Galleria AARNI: Located in the Tapiola area, Galleria AARNI showcases Finnish design and contemporary art, offering unique pieces from local artists.

Address: Leppavaarankatu 3 9 3. Krs, 02600 Espoo

Heureka Shop: Inside the Finnish Science Centre Heureka, this shop offers science-related toys, games, and educational materials for all ages.

Address: Tiedepuisto 1, 01300 Vantaa

Sipoonkorpi Visitor Centre Shop: Situated in the Sipoonkorpi National Park, this shop offers outdoor gear, maps, and local products, catering to nature enthusiasts exploring the park.

Mathildedal Art & Design Boutiques: In the Mathildedal Ironworks Village, various boutiques showcase local art, design, and crafts, providing a unique shopping experience.

Moomin Shop Naantali: Located in Naantali's Old Town, this shop specializes in Moomin-themed products, including books, toys, and souvenirs inspired by the beloved Moomin characters.

Address: Mannerheiminkatu 3, 21100 Naantali

Pallavasidami: Situated in the city center, this shop offers a selection of locally made crafts, gifts, and souvenirs, showcasing the talents of Uusikaupunki artisans.

Address: Koulukatu 11B, Uusikaupunki

Accommodation

Name	Information	Address
Hotel Korpilampi (Espoo)	A comfortable hotel surrounded by nature, offering a peaceful retreat near Nuuksio National Park.	Korpilammentie 5, 02970 Espoo
GLO Hotel Sello (Espoo)	A stylish hotel in Leppävaara, providing modern amenities and convenient access to shopping and cultural attractions.	Leppavaarankatu 1, 02600 Espoo
GLO Hotel Helsinki Airport (Vantaa)	Located near Helsinki-Vantaa Airport, this hotel offers a convenient stay with modern facilities.	Terminaali, Lentoasemantie, 01530 Vantaa
Forenom Aparthotel Vantaa Tikkurila (Vantaa)	Situated in a central location, this hotel provides comfortable apartments and is close to the Heureka Science Musuem.	Varitehtaankatu 8, 01300 Vantaa
Hotel Pariisin Ville (Porvoo)	A charming hotel in Porvoo's Old Town, providing a taste of history through its atmosphere and comfortable accommodations.	Jokikatu 43, 06100 Porvoo
Haikko Manor & Spa (Porvoo)	Situated in a beautiful manor setting, this hotel offers a luxurious experience with spa facilities and scenic surroundings.	Haikkoontie 114, 06400 Porvoo

Kirkkonummi	In Kirkkonummi, you can find apartments and vacation rentals on websites such as Airbnb, but there are no hotels there as of the writing of this book. (https://www.airbnb.com/kirkkonummi-finland/stays)	
Hotelli Uninen Loviisa (Loviisa)	Located in the center of the town, this hotel offers you a comfortable stay with a variety of amenities.	Brandensteinink atu 17, 07900 Loviisa
Ulrikanhovi (Loviisa)	Situated near the city center, this hotel provides comfortable rooms with a wonderful view.	Kuhlefeltinkatu 35, 07940 Loviisa
Joensuun Tilan Paarakennus (Sipoo)	Located in Söderkulla, this hotel set in a former farmhouse offers comfortable rooms and is near Sipoonkorpi National Park.	Joensuun raitti 58, 01150 Söderkulla
Original Sokos Hotel Rikala (Salo)	Situated on the banks of Uskelanjoki river, this relaxed hotel is near the main attractions you may want to visit.	Asemakatu 15, 24100 Salo
Rock Hotel Salo (Salo)	Rock Hotel Salo offers spacious rooms and multiple amenities. It is also located near popular attractions in the city.	Asemakatu 5, 24100 Salo
Naantali Spa Hotel (Naantali)	One of the largest spa hotels in the Nordic countries, offering wellness facilities and a seaside location.	Matkailijantie 2, 21100 Naantali

Hotel Palo (Naantali)	A cozy hotel in Naantali's Old Town, providing a traditional atmosphere and proximity to local attractions.	Luostarinkatu 12, 21100 Naantali
Hotelli Havu (Uusikaupun ki)	A comfortable hotel in Uusikaupunki offering modern amenities in a convenient location.	Levysepankatu 1, 23500 Uusikaupunki
Hotelli Aittaranta (Uusikaupun ki)	This hotel offers modern, comfortable rooms with a variety of amenities with restaurants nearby.	Aittaranta 2, 23500 Uusikaupunki

These cities have something for everyone. If you are looking to experience a rich local culture and community spirit, then these are your best choices. You should have no trouble engaging with the friendly locals. These places are a mix of historical treasures and natural wonders for curious travelers. The amazing architectural history will undoubtedly leave all history buffs beyond satisfied.

Chapter 5: Lapland (Lappi)

Lapland, known as Lappi in Finnish, is a fascinating region in the northernmost part of Finland, stretching across the Arctic Circle. Popular for its breathtaking natural landscapes, unique indigenous culture, and the magical allure of the Northern Lights, Lapland has become a popular destination for travelers seeking a one-of-a-kind experience.

Brief Historical Background

Lapland has been home to the indigenous Sámi people, who have inhabited the region for thousands of years. The Sámi are a distinct group with their own languages, traditions, and livelihoods centered on reindeer herding and fishing. While modernization and

Lapland on the map.[34]

global influences have changed the cultural landscape of the region, the Sámi culture still shines bright, portraying the true identity of Lapland.

The region has a rich history influenced by various past events and held strategic importance during World War II. Lapland witnessed various military operations, like the German withdrawal from the area in 1944, reshaping the local landscape and communities.

Geographically, Lapland's landscape is dominated by vast expanses of wilderness, including dense forests, rolling hills, and numerous lakes. The region experiences extreme seasonal variations, with long, harsh winters and the enchanting phenomenon of the Midnight Sun during the summer months. This unique environment has shaped the way of life in Lapland, with outdoor activities like hiking, skiing, and snowmobiling being popular among both locals and visitors.

In addition to its natural wonders, Lapland is recognized as the official hometown of Santa Claus. The Arctic Circle passes through the village of Rovaniemi, which hosts Santa Claus Village—a magical place where you can meet Santa, cross the Arctic Circle, and experience the festive atmosphere year-round. You'll learn more about these places of interest later on in the chapter.

Lapland, Finland.[35]

Lapland is indeed a captivating destination that seamlessly blends history, culture, and nature, offering a truly immersive experience for those who want to explore the pristine landscapes and embrace its distinctive way of life. Whether seeking the enchantment of the Northern Lights, the thrill of winter sports, or a glimpse into the indigenous Sámi culture, Lapland promises an unforgettable journey into the heart of the Arctic.

Main Attractions

Rovaniemi

Santa Claus Village

Rovaniemi is the official hometown of Santa Claus. Here, you can meet Santa Claus himself every day of the year. The village is designed to capture the enchanting spirit of Christmas, creating a magical atmosphere with Christmas-themed activities, shops, and even Santa's post office.

As of the writing of this book, Santa Claus Village is open 24 hours every day. However, please make sure to double-check the opening hours online should there be any slight changes to their schedules.

Address: 96930 Rovaniemi

Arktikum

Arktikum is a museum and science center in Rovaniemi which beautifully showcases the Arctic life and the history of Lapland. Exhibits represent the region's unique environment, wildlife, and the cultural heritage of the indigenous Sámi people. It can be an educational and immersive experience, deepening your understanding of the Arctic.

As of the writing of this book, the opening hours are every day from 9 am to 6 pm and closed on Monday. However, please make sure to double-check the opening hours online should there be any slight changes to their schedule.

Address: Pohjoisranta 4, 96200 Rovaniemi

Inari

Siida Sámi Museum and Nature Centre

Inari, known as the heart of Sámi culture in Finland, is home to the Siida Sámi Museum and Nature Centre. This museum provides you with a deep dive into the local indigenous heritage. Siida showcases Sámi traditions, culture, and the unique Arctic nature that defines the region. Exhibits include artifacts, traditional Sámi crafts, and information about the Arctic environment. If you are a history nerd, add this to your list.

As of the writing of this book, the opening hours are Tuesday to Sunday from 10 am to 6 pm. However, please make sure to double-check the opening hours online should there be any slight changes to their schedule.

Address: Inarintie 46, 99870 Inari

Siida Sámi Museum.[36]

Lake Inari

Lake Inari is the largest lake in Lapland and a prominent feature of the region. The lake offers stunning views and opportunities for water-based activities like boating and fishing. The serene atmosphere around the lake provides a peaceful escape, and the surrounding wilderness adds to the overall charm of the area. You can either indulge in fishing or boating activities or opt for a calm spot near the lake to enjoy nature at its finest.

You can visit Lake Inari at any time during your trip.

Lake Inari.[37]

Northern Lights

Inari is situated in a prime location for spotting the Northern Lights, also known as the Aurora Borealis. The dark arctic nights during certain times of the year create a perfect backdrop for witnessing this mesmerizing natural phenomenon. It's an ideal destination for those seeking a serene and unspoiled natural environment.

Northern Lights.[38]

Sodankylä
Old Wooden Church

Old Wooden Church.[39]

Sodankylä is celebrated for its Old Wooden Church, a remarkable construction marvel dating back to the 17th century. This architectural gem is a highlight of the region's rich cultural heritage. You can step into the past as you go through the well-preserved interiors and exteriors of this historical church, exploring the craftsmanship and religious practices of bygone eras.

As of the writing of this book, the Old Wooden Church is temporarily closed. However, it is worth looking at from the outside, which you can do at any time during your trip.

Address: Sodankylä hautausmaa, Kirkkotie 1, 99600 Sodankylä

Kemi

SnowCastle of Kemi

Kemi boasts a one-of-a-kind attraction, the SnowCastle of Kemi, which holds the title of the largest snow fort globally and is reconstructed each winter. This architectural marvel combines the enchantment of a snow fort with artistic and imaginative designs. Explore the snow sculptures, intricate corridors, and themed rooms, experiencing the magic of this mesmerizing winter wonderland.

As of the writing of this book, the opening hours are Monday to Saturday from 7 am to 8 pm, and Sunday from 8 am to 6 pm. However, please make sure to double-check the opening hours online should there be any slight changes to their schedule.

Address: Lumilinnankatu 15, 94100 Kemi.

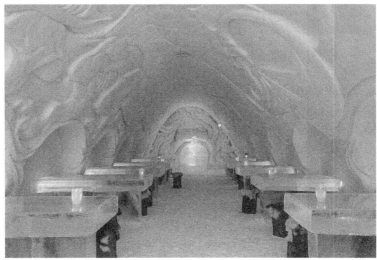

The SnowCastle of Kemi.[40]

Gemstone Gallery

Kemi offers a cultural gem in the form of the Gemstone Gallery, where you can marvel at replicas of the crown jewels of Europe.

As of the writing of this book, the opening hours are Monday to Friday from 10 am to 5 pm, Saturday from 10 am to 3 pm, and closed on Sunday. However, please make sure to double-check the opening hours online should there be any slight changes to their schedule.

Address: Marina Takalon katu 3, 94100 Kemi.

The Gemstone Gallery[41]

Kittilä

Pallas-Yllästunturi National Park

Kittilä provides access to the stunning Pallas-Yllästunturi National Park, a natural gem known for its clean air, extensive mires, and scenic hiking routes. This national park is a paradise for nature lovers where you can hike through ancient forests, cross crystal-clear streams, and ascend to the top of fjells for breathtaking panoramic views for an immersive experience in the lap of the Finnish wilderness.

As of the writing of this book, the Pallas-Yllästunturi National Park is open 24 hours every day. However, please make sure to double-check the opening hours online should there be any slight changes to their schedule.

Utsjoki

Utsjoki, being the northernmost municipality in Finland, is another area inhabited by the Sámi people. The region preserves the rich cultural heritage of the Sámi, allowing guests to engage with traditional practices, explore unique arts and crafts, and gain insights into the community's way of life and the indigenous heritage of Utsjoki.

This municipality is recognized for its stark and beautiful *fjells* (mountains). These fjells, paired with breathtaking scenery, are perfect for outdoor activities like hiking, skiing, and snowmobiling.

Kevo Strict Nature Reserve

Utsjoki is home to the Kevo Strict Nature Reserve, a protected area with unique biodiversity and an untouched habitat. The reserve features deep ravines, meandering rivers, and Arctic tundra, making it an ecologically significant area for nature enthusiasts to explore. Hiking trails wind through the reserve, immersing you in unspoiled nature.

As of the writing of this book, the Kevo Strict Nature Reserve is open 24 hours every day. However, please make sure to double-check the opening hours online should there be any slight changes to their schedule.

Address: Kevontie 444, 99980 Utsjoki.

Natural Phenomena

Utsjoki's extreme northern location brings about natural phenomena that captivate throughout the year. During the summer months, the region experiences the midnight sun, where the sun remains visible around the clock. In contrast, the polar nights in winter bring extended periods of darkness. Also, in Utsjoki, chances are high to witness the Northern Lights, with the expansive Arctic sky serving as a canvas for the dancing colors of the aurora borealis.

Enontekiö

Vast Wilderness for Outdoor Activities

Enontekiö, aptly named the "birthplace of rivers," features untouched areas, providing an ideal setting for a variety of outdoor activities. You can enjoy trekking, fishing, and skiing in the unspoiled landscapes. The region's alluring nature, with its rivers, lakes, and snowy terrain, is an excellent option for anyone seeking adventure and tranquility.

Panoramic Views from Numerous Fjells

Enontekiö is dotted with numerous fjells and breathtaking landscapes. These elevated vantage points are perfect for enjoying the Arctic scenery, making them popular destinations for hikers and nature lovers. The varied topography gives visitors a diverse range of trekking experiences.

Did You Know?

Enontekiö is not only known for its natural beauty and Sámi culture but also for being the birthplace of Nils-Aslak Valkeapää, a highly regarded Sámi writer, musician, and artist. Valkeapää, often referred to as Áillohaš, made significant contributions to preserving and promoting Sámi culture through his works. His legacy continues to influence and inspire those interested in the indigenous heritage of the region.

Muonio

Olos for Winter Activities

Outdoor enthusiasts can go to Olos for cross-country skiing and snowshoeing. This location provides well-groomed trails and snow-covered landscapes, creating a perfect place for sports adventures surrounded by nature.

Address: Oloshotellintie 25, 99300 Muonio.

Spectacles of Nature

Muonio's location above the Arctic Circle makes it an excellent spot for witnessing the spectacles of the Northern Lights and the midnight sun. The dark winter nights create the perfect setting for the aurora borealis, while the summer months bring the enchanting phenomenon of the midnight sun, where daylight persists around the clock. These natural displays add a magical touch to the Muonio experience.

Transportation in Lapland

Lapland, with its vast and remote landscapes, has diverse transportation options to explore its unique attractions. Whether you're heading to the official hometown of Santa Claus in Rovaniemi or want to spend nights in the wilderness of Inari or Utsjoki, you won't encounter a problem in Lapland if you plan properly.

Air Travel

Rovaniemi Airport: It's the primary gateway to Lapland, connecting the region to major Finnish cities and international destinations.

Ivalo Airport: For those heading to Inari or Utsjoki, Ivalo Airport is a key hub. It provides access to the northernmost parts of Lapland and offers regular flights from Helsinki.

Local Airports

Kittilä Airport: Located near Levi, Kittilä Airport facilitates easy access to one of Lapland's most popular ski resorts.

Enontekiö Airport: For travelers exploring Enontekiö and its untouched lands, the local airport provides convenient connections.

Train Travel

Rovaniemi Railway Station: Lapland is well-connected by train and is a major railway hub for the region. The Santa Claus Express, among other trains, links Lapland to southern Finland.

Kolari Railway Station: Situated near Levi, Kolari Railway Station is another convenient option for those heading to the western part of Lapland.

Bus Services

Lapland has a well-developed network of buses that connect various towns and villages. It's a cost-effective means of transportation, offering scenic routes and the flexibility to explore multiple destinations. Long-distance coach services are available that connect Lapland to major cities in Finland.

Car Rentals

Several car rental agencies operate in major towns and airports. If visiting during the winter months, it's essential to book in advance if you are planning a road trip.

Local Transportation

Taxis are available in major towns and cities, making your traveling in urban areas stress-free. In certain regions, traditional transportation methods like husky sleighs and reindeer sleighs are commonly used, adding a unique experience.

Ferries

For those exploring coastal areas like Kemi, ferries and cruises offer a scenic way to experience Lapland. Icebreaker cruises are a highlight, providing a memorable journey through frozen waters.

Cycling

Bike Rentals: In milder seasons, cycling becomes a popular mode of transportation, especially in towns like Rovaniemi.

Winter Transfers

In winter, snowmobile transfers are available in some areas, providing an adventurous way to travel through snowy landscapes.

Experiences in Lapland

Midnight Sun Film Festival (Sodankylä)

Sodankylä takes center stage each year as it hosts the Midnight Sun Film Festival, an international gathering that celebrates cinema and welcomes movie enthusiasts. Set against the backdrop of the Arctic Circle's continuous daylight during the summer months, this festival provides a unique cinematic experience where film screenings blend seamlessly with the surreal atmosphere of the midnight sun.

Icebreaker Cruise (Kemi)

For a thrilling adventure, visitors to Kemi can hop on an icebreaker cruise. These excursions allow guests to see the powerful icebreakers in action as they break through the frozen sea.

Floating Swimming Experience (Kemi)

This invigorating activity involves taking a dip in icy waters while floating, protected by a special thermal suit. It's a thrilling and memorable way to immerse oneself in the extreme Arctic conditions while remaining safe and buoyant.

Levi Ski Resort (Kittilä)

Kittilä is a haven for ski enthusiasts, being home to Levi, Finland's most popular ski resort. Levi offers excellent slopes to skiers of all levels. Beyond the thrill of skiing, the resort has ongoing activities, restaurants, and bars. Luxurious accommodations add to the overall appeal, making Levi a go-to destination for those seeking a perfect blend of winter sports and relaxation.

Address: Hissitie 8, 99130 Kittilä.

Husky and Reindeer Sleigh Rides (Rovaniemi)

For a genuinely Arctic experience, you can enjoy husky and reindeer sleigh rides. These traditional modes of transportation allow tourists to explore the snowy wilderness authentically and memorably. It's an opportunity to connect with the local culture and the animals that have been integral to the way of life in Lapland.

Husky Safaris (Hetta)

The town of Hetta in Enontekiö stands out as a hub for husky safaris, allowing you to experience the thrill of dog sledding through the snowy landscapes. Additionally, Hetta is home to the distinctive Enontekiö Church, known for its unique architecture. The church adds a cultural touch to the area, making it a point of interest for those exploring the region.

Where to Eat in Lapland

Lapland's culinary landscape seamlessly weaves together traditional Sámi flavors and contemporary Nordic influences. From intimate local eateries to sophisticated fine dining establishments, explore the authentic gastronomic experiences that Lapland has to offer.

Name	Information	Address
Nili Restaurant (Rovaniemi)	Nili specializes in modern Sámi cuisine, featuring dishes that showcase the richness of Lapland's natural ingredients. Reindeer, fish, and local berries take center stage in contemporary Sámi creations. The restaurant's inviting ambiance and extensive wine selection enhance the dining experience.	Valtakatu 20, 96200 Rovaniemi
Ravintola Roka Street Bistro (Rovaniemi)	Ravintola Roka Street Bistro offers authentic Lappi street food as well as a twist on authentic Finnish classics. The restaurant's cozy interior and impressive wine	Ainonkatu 3LH2, 96200 Rovaniemi

	selection create an inviting setting for indulging in Finnish culinary delights.	
Gustav Kitchen and Bar (Rovaniemi)	Gustav Kitchen and Bar is a restaurant beloved by locals. This restaurant offers delicious food from International cuisines with a delightful atmosphere and great service.	Koskikatu 12, 96200 Rovaniemi
Aurora Village Restaurant (Inari)	Overlooking the Northern Lights, Aurora Village Restaurant provides a unique dining experience with a menu that emphasizes modern Nordic cuisine. Local and seasonal ingredients are at the forefront of dishes, creating a perfect harmony with the captivating surroundings.	Aurorakuja 38, 99800 Inari
Sarrit (Inari)	Sarrit is the place for those seeking authentic Sámi and local delicacies. The menu, featuring reindeer and fish, captures the essence of Lapland's traditional flavors. The cozy atmosphere adds to the charm of this culinary gem.	Inarintie 46, 99870 Inari
Ravintola RuusuSola	At Ravintola RuusuSola, enjoy a buffet of food with a	Jäämerentie 28, 99600 Sodankylä

(Sodankylä)	menu that changes daily. Check the menu before your visit to enjoy lunch at this comfortable restaurant that offers Finnish dishes with a twist.	
Saamen Kammi (Kittilä)	Specializing in Lappish cuisine, Saamen Kammi serves dishes like sautéed reindeer and smoked salmon. The cozy interior has a campfire in the middle of the restaurant and you can watch your food being prepared over an open fire.	Kätkänrannantie 2, 99130 Kittilä
Utsjoki Arctic Resort Restaurant (Utsjoki)	Experience a blend of local and international flavors at Utsjoki Arctic Resort Restaurant. With panoramic views, the restaurant provides an ideal setting to savor traditional Sámi delicacies and immerse in the Lapland dining experience.	Nuorgamintie 91, 99980 Utsjoki

Shopping Guide

Lapland offers a unique shopping experience, blending traditional craftsmanship with contemporary Nordic designs. From Sámi handicrafts to locally sourced products, here's your guide to finding Arctic treasures in the charming shops and markets of Lapland.

Sámi Handicrafts

Look for traditional items like duodji, which includes intricately designed jewelry, clothing, and crafts adorned with Sámi symbols. Local markets, Sámi craft shops, and cultural centers are excellent places to find these handmade treasures.

Lappish Leather Products

Reindeer leather goods like gloves, hats, and accessories, as well as Lappish leather items like wallets and belts, are an option if you want to take back some practical souvenirs. These high-quality products can often be found in local leather workshops, markets, and specialty souvenir shops.

Lappish Food and Beverages

Bring the flavors of Lapland home by purchasing local delicacies like cloudberry products, smoked reindeer meat, Sámi cheese (gáhkko), and traditional Lappish berry liqueurs. Visit local food markets, grocery stores, and specialty shops to explore the culinary delights of the region.

Lappish Handmade Textiles

Experience the art of traditional Sámi weaving by investing in handwoven textiles, including the iconic Sámi gákti (clothing) and beautifully crafted blankets, rugs, and scarves made from natural materials. Seek out local textile workshops, craft markets, and specialty stores for these unique items.

Northern Lights Souvenirs

Capture the magic of the aurora borealis with Northern Lights-themed souvenirs. Look for art prints, clothing, and home decor items inspired by this celestial phenomenon. Gift shops, tourist centers, and art galleries often feature a variety of Northern Lights-inspired merchandise.

Sports and Leisure Activities

Winter Sports (Rovaniemi)

Rovaniemi offers various winter sports activities, making it a hub for adventure seekers. You can engage in activities like skiing, snowboarding, and other winter sports, taking advantage of the snowy landscape. The region's winter wonderland provides a picturesque backdrop for these activities.

Golfing in Summer (Kittilä)

As the snow gives way to the vibrant greens of summer, Kittilä becomes a destination for golf enthusiasts. The town offers golfing facilities, allowing you to enjoy the picturesque landscapes and the extended daylight hours characteristic of the Finnish summer. It's a unique experience to trade the ski slopes for the golf course, highlighting the diverse recreational opportunities available in Kittilä.

Accommodations in Lapland

Rovaniemi

Santa's Igloos Arctic Circle (Rovaniemi)

These unique accommodations consist of glass-roofed igloos situated near the Arctic Circle. Guests can enjoy panoramic views of the Northern Lights right from the comfort of their igloo. Each igloo is equipped with modern amenities, ensuring a comfortable stay in the magical surroundings.

Address: Joulumaankuja 8, 96930 Rovaniemi.

Arctic Light Hotel (Rovaniemi)

Located in the heart of Rovaniemi, the Arctic Light Hotel has a stylish and modern atmosphere. Guests can easily explore Rovaniemi's attractions, and the hotel often organizes activities like the Northern Lights tours for an immersive Lapland experience.

Address: Valtakatu 18, 96200 Rovaniemi.

Inari

Wilderness Hotel Inari (Inari)

Situated in a forested area by lake Inari, Wilderness Hotel Inari combines traditional Sámi charm with modern amenities. Guests can enjoy views of the river and the surrounding wilderness. The hotel is known for its warm hospitality and locally inspired cuisine, offering a genuine taste of Lapland.

Address: Inarintie 2, 99870 Inari.

Inari Igloos, Aurora Cabins (Inari)

This accommodation option provides cozy cabins and igloos in Lapland's serene nature. Guests can view the Northern Lights right outside their accommodation. It is an ideal retreat for those seeking a peaceful vacation.

Address: Inarintie 2, 99870 Inari.

Kemi

Guests can choose to stay in snow or glass igloos, allowing them to sleep under the Northern Lights or enjoy the snowscape. The SnowHotel is rebuilt every winter, offering a magical and unforgettable stay.

SnowHotelAddress: Lumilinnankatu 15, 94100 Kemi.

Levi (Kittilä)

Levi Hotel Spa (Kittilä)

Levi Hotel Spa is a family-friendly option located near Levi's ski slopes. The hotel features spa facilities, comfortable rooms, and various activities for both adults and children. Its convenient location makes it a popular choice for families looking to enjoy winter sports and outdoor adventures.

Address: Levintie 1590, 99130 Levi.

Golden Crown Levin Iglut (Kittilä)

For a premium Northern Lights experience, Golden Crown Levin Iglut offers luxury glass igloos. Guests can enjoy the magical light displays from the warmth and comfort of their private igloo, complete with modern amenities and stunning panoramic views.

Address: Harjatie 2, 99130 Kittilä.

Muonio

Lapland Hotels Olos (Muonio)

Lapland Hotels Olos is a resort-style accommodation offering a range of outdoor activities, including skiing and hiking. The hotel provides comfortable rooms, wellness facilities, and a restaurant with Lappish cuisine. Its location near Olos ski slopes makes it convenient for winter sports enthusiasts.

Address: Oloshotellintie 25, 99300 Muonio.

Torassieppi Eco Reindeer Resort (Muonio)

This option offers cozy cottages on a reindeer farm where guests can learn about reindeer herding, enjoy the tranquil surroundings, and even participate in winter activities like sleigh rides.

Address: Torassiepintie 212, 99300 Muonio.

Utsjoki

Utsjoki Arctic Resort (Utsjoki)

Utsjoki Arctic Resort provides a range of accommodations, including riverside cabins and wilderness rooms. Guests can immerse themselves in the Arctic surroundings, participate in outdoor activities, and enjoy the peaceful ambiance of Utsjoki.

Address: Nuorgamintie 91, 99980 Utsjoki.

Chapter 6: Kainuu and Karelia

Kainuu and Karelia reflect the spirit of the Finnish people, shaped by a history of cultural interplay, geographical significance, and a deep connection to nature. In this chapter, you'll explore the unique characteristics, cultural nuances, and natural wonders that make this region a captivating destination to visit.

Kainuu, Finland.[42]

Brief Historical Background

Kainuu

Kainuu has been shaped by its proximity to Russia and Sweden, with influences from both cultures evident in its traditions. The region has been a hub for trade and cultural exchange, contributing to its unique identity. With vast forests, pristine lakes, and a captivating landscape, Kainuu is an excellent destination for those seeking tranquility and a connection to nature.

Kainuu on the map.[43]

Karelia

Karelia is a region steeped in history and characterized by its unique cultural heritage. The Finnish part of Karelia is known for its mesmerizing natural habitats, including the stunning Lake Ladoga, dense forests, and meandering rivers. The history of Karelia is filled with tales of resilience, as the region has witnessed shifts in borders and populations over the centuries. With a distinct blend of Finnish and Karelian influences, this area is a treasure trove of natural beauty and cultural richness.

Karelia on the map.[44]

Main Attractions

Kainuu Attractions
Kajaani Castle (Kajaani)

Kajaani Castle.[45]

Along the banks of the Kajaani River, you'll find the Kajaani Castle, a historical gem that dates back to the 17th century. The castle is used as a cultural hub to host events, concerts, and exhibitions throughout the year. With its artistic setting and rich historical backdrop, Kajaani Castle invites you to explore the region's heritage and immerse yourself in its vibrant cultural scene.

As of the writing of this book, Kajaani Castle is open 24 hours daily. However, please make sure to double-check the opening hours online should there be any slight changes to their schedule.

Address: Brahenkatu 1, 87100 Kajaani.

Did You Know?

Kajaani Castle was a significant site during the Greater Wrath, a conflict between Russia and Sweden, and has since evolved into a symbol of resilience during hard times.

Hiidenportti National Park (Sotkamo)

Hiidenportti National Park is a wilderness sanctuary with a rugged landscape and the peculiar Gate of the Devil rock formation. The park's name, translating to the Gate of the Devil, adds a touch of folklore to the natural beauty. Offering hiking trails and birdwatching opportunities, Hiidenportti National Park is a serene escape into the heart of untouched nature.

As of the writing of this book, Hiidenportti National Park is open 24 hours every day. However, please make sure to double-check the opening hours online should there be any slight changes to their schedule.

Address: Hiidenportintie 86, 88600 Sotkamo.

Did You Know?

Hiidenportti National Park is home to rare plant species and is a prime location for birdwatching, making it a popular spot for nature lovers and ornithologists.

Lake Oulujärvi (Sotkamo)

Lake Oulujärvi.[46]

Lake Oulujärvi, in the scenic Kainuu region of eastern Finland, is the fourth-largest lake in the country. It covers an expansive area of approximately 928 square kilometers and includes crystal-clear waters, numerous islands, and forests, creating the perfect setting for various recreational activities. From boating and fishing in the warmer months to ice fishing and winter sports during the colder season, Lake Oulujärvi can be visited in any season. The lake's shores are adorned with historical sites and villages, making the area an integral part of the local heritage.

As of the writing of the book, you can visit Lake Oulujärvi at any time during your trip. However, please make sure to double-check the opening hours online should there be any slight changes to their schedule.

Did You Know?

Submerged in the lake's depths are ancient burial sites known as kettle holes, which date back thousands of years. These underwater archaeological findings provide insights into the early human settlement around the Lake Oulujärvi region.

Karelia Attractions

Joensuu Art Museum (Joensuu)

Joensuu Art Museum.[47]

The Joensuu Art Museum, also known as Joensuun Taidemuseo in Finnish, is an important cultural hub in the city of Joensuu. The museum showcases a diverse collection of visual arts, including paintings, sculptures, and other forms of contemporary and traditional art. It's a platform for both local and international artists, making the cultural scene in the region vibrant. The museum building itself has unique architectural features, and its exhibition spaces are designed to provide a dynamic and engaging environment for visitors.

As of the writing of this book, Joensuu Art Museum is closed for renovations until 2026.

Address: Kirkkokatu 23, 9010 Joensuu.

Did You Know?

The Joensuu Art Museum actively engages with the community by organizing various events, workshops, and educational programs. These initiatives promote arts, encourage creativity, and provide a space for dialogue between artists and the public. The museum's commitment to community involvement enhances its role as a cultural and educational resource for Joensuu residents and visitors alike.

Joensuu Arboretum (Joensuu)

The Joensuu Arboretum is a green oasis in the heart of Joensuu. It's a place of both leisure and education, showcasing a diverse collection of plants, flowers, and trees. The gardens exhibit various species, including both native and exotic plants, organized in thematic sections. You can enjoy strolls through well-maintained paths, learn about different plant species, and appreciate the beauty of nature.

As of the writing of this book, you can visit the Joensuu Arboretum at any time during your trip. However, please make sure to double-check the opening hours online should there be any slight changes to their schedule.

Did You Know?

This arboretum is not only aesthetically pleasing but also serve as valuable resources for research and conservation. Many botanical gardens, including Joensuu's, participate actively in initiatives to protect endangered plant species, conduct studies on plant biology, and contribute to the broader scientific understanding of plant life. They also often organize events, workshops, and educational programs to engage the local community and promote environmental awareness.

Koli National Park

Koli National, with its mesmerizing landscapes and panoramic views from Ukko-Koli Hill, is a haven for hikers with its scenic trails, including the Herajärvi Circuit. The Finnish national epic, Kalevala, drew inspiration from the captivating landscapes of Koli, adding an extra layer of allure to this enchanting region.

As of the writing of this book, you can visit Koli National Park at any time during your trip. However, please make sure to double-check the opening hours online should there be any slight changes to their schedule.

Address: Yla-Kolintie 38, 83960 Lieksa.

Did You Know?

Koli National Park is a designated Dark Sky Park, offering unparalleled opportunities for stargazing and experiencing the magic of the night sky.

Valamo Monastery

Valamo Monastery.[48]

Situated on an island in Lake Juurikkaselka, the Valamo Monastery is a tranquil retreat that unfolds the spiritual history of Karelia. Originally established in Russian Karelia in the 14th century, the monastery was relocated to Finland, retaining its traditional Orthodox architecture. The Valamo Monastery complex includes a museum and chapel, providing a serene experience surrounded by nature.

As of the writing of this book the opening hours are every day from 9 am to 9 pm. However, please make sure to double-check the opening hours online should there be any slight changes to their schedule.

Address: Valamontie 42, 79850 Uusi Valamo.

Did You Know?

The Valamo Monastery is renowned for its centuries-old tradition of producing exquisite icon paintings, showcasing the artistic heritage of the Orthodox Church.

Kitee Zoo

Kitee Zoo is a wildlife park showcasing various animals, including both native and exotic species. The zoo is known for its focus on animal welfare and conservation efforts. You can visit the park to see animals in spacious and naturalistic enclosures, promoting a more ethical and educational approach to zookeeping. The zoo has a diverse range of animals, such as mammals, birds, and reptiles.

As of the writing of this book, the opening hours are every day from 10 am to 5 pm. However, please make sure to double-check the opening hours online should there be any slight changes to their schedule.

Address: Pajarinniementie 1, 82430 Puhos.

Joensuu Market Square

Joensuu's Market Square is a vibrant hub where locals and visitors converge to experience the city's cultural diversity. Hosting a variety of events and featuring market stalls offering local produce, crafts, and Karelian delicacies, the square is a lively reflection of Joensuu's communal spirit.

As of the writing of this book, you can visit Joensuu Market Square at any time during your trip. However, please make sure to double-check the opening hours online should there be any slight changes to their schedule.

Address: Joensunn tori, 80100 Joensuu.

Did You Know?

Joensuu Market Square transforms into a winter wonderland during the festive season, adorned with lights and decorations, creating a magical atmosphere for holiday celebrations.

Lake Saimaa

Lake Saimaa.[49]

Lake Saimaa is the largest lake in Finland and one of the largest in Europe. Located in the southeastern part of the country, Lake Saimaa is a stunning labyrinth of waterways, islands, and peninsulas. Its vast expanse covers several municipalities, including Lappeenranta, Savonlinna, and Mikkeli. The lake, known for its clear waters and picturesque surroundings, is a popular destination for boating, fishing, and nature enthusiasts. The Saimaa region around the lake offers a unique blend of charming lakeside villages and cultural attractions. You can also visit historical sites like Olavinlinna Castle in Savonlinna and enjoy the tranquility of the Finnish Lakeland.

As of the writing of this book, you can visit Lake Saimaa at any time during your trip. However, please make sure to double-check the opening hours online should there be any changes to their schedule.

Did You Know?

Lake Saimaa is the home of Saimaa ringed seals, one of the rarest and most endangered seal species in the world. The seals are adapted to freshwater environments and can be observed basking on rocks or ice.

Karelian Landscapes

The Karelian landscapes refer to the natural beauty found in the historical region of Karelia, which spans parts of Finland and Russia. With vast forests, lakes, and gently rolling hills, Karelia showcases the quintessential beauty of Northern Europe. Karelia holds cultural significance, with traditional wooden architecture, Orthodox churches, and folklore adding to the charm of the landscape. You can enjoy outdoor activities, including hiking, berry picking, and exploring the unique blend of nature and culture.

Did You Know?

Karelia is famous for its traditional music and poetry, known as *rune singing* or *runo-song*. This form of oral poetry has been recognized by UNESCO as a Masterpiece of the Oral and Intangible Heritage of Humanity, highlighting the cultural richness of the Karelian people.

Transportation in Kainuu and Karelia

Exploring Kainuu and Karelia is made seamless by a range of transportation options that offer both convenience and the opportunity to soak in scenic landscapes.

Car Rentals

Major cities and airports offer several car rental options, allowing you to start your road trips across sprawling landscapes right away. Some car rental agencies in the region also provide winter-ready vehicles equipped with snow tires and heating systems, ensuring a comfortable journey during the colder months.

The roadways in Kainuu and Karelia offer captivating drives, especially during autumn when the landscapes transform into a display of vibrant colors. Likewise, the journey through Koli National Park and the Kajaani region presents enchanting views of forests, lakes, and hills.

Buses

Buses connect major cities and towns in the region, making them a cost-effective and environmentally friendly mode of transportation. They are a convenient option for both short-distance travel within cities and longer journeys between regions.

Trains

The railway network in Finland extends into Kainuu and Karelia, offering efficient and comfortable train travel. The train journey from Joensuu to Koli, for example, provides scenic views of the surrounding countryside.

Airports

The region has airports in cities like Kajaani and Joensuu, hosting domestic and limited international flights. Air travel is a quick way to cover longer distances within and around Kainuu and Karelia.

Cycling

Cycling is an eco-friendly way to explore towns, cities, and nature trails. Many areas have well-maintained cycling paths, and some accommodations provide bicycles for guests.

Did You Know?

You can explore the Koli National Park on just a bicycle. You can navigate the trails at your own pace and take in the beauty of the surroundings.

Boats and Ferries

In Karelia, especially around the lakes and water bodies, you can find boats and ferries. These waterways connect to islands, nature reserves, and cultural sites.

Some boat services operate themed cruises, combining transportation with cultural and historical narratives for a comprehensive exploration.

Experiences in Kainuu and Karelia

Travel into the heart of Kainuu and Karelia with curated experiences that go beyond conventional sightseeing. From cultural events to nature-themed excursions, these immersive encounters offer a deeper connection to the essence of these captivating regions.

Folklore Festivals in Karelia

Dive into Karelian traditions and folklore by attending local festivals that showcase traditional music, dance, and crafts. These events often take place in charming towns, offering an authentic glimpse into the region's cultural heritage.

Did You Know?

Some festivals feature interactive workshops where visitors can actively participate in traditional crafts and activities.

Kajaani Poetry Week

Celebrate the literary legacy of Kajaani during the annual Poetry Week. The event brings poets, writers, and literature enthusiasts together for readings, discussions, and performances, creating a vibrant cultural atmosphere.

Did You Know?

Kajaani's Poetry Week often includes events in unique locations, such as historic sites and outdoor settings, enhancing the poetic ambiance.

Birdwatching Excursions

Go on guided birdwatching tours in Hiidenportti National Park, where expert naturalists lead you through diverse habitats. Discover the region's rich birdlife, including rare species that call the park home.

Did You Know?

Hiidenportti National Park is a haven for birdwatchers, offering a chance to spot elusive species like the Siberian Jay and the Black Grouse.

Karelian Cooking Classes

Engage your taste buds with Karelian cuisine through hands-on cooking classes. Learn to prepare local delicacies such as Karelian pasties and fish dishes, and gain insight into the region's culinary traditions.

Did You Know?

Cooking classes often include visits to local markets, taking you to source fresh ingredients and connect with regional producers.

Vuokatti's Arctic Spa Experience

Indulge in a unique spa experience in Vuokatti, where the Arctic environment sets the backdrop for relaxation. Enjoy traditional Finnish sauna sessions, ice swimming, and wellness treatments inspired by the purity of Lapland.

Paddling Adventures in Lake Pielinen

Navigate the crystal-clear waters of Lake Pielinen on a guided paddling adventure. Discover hidden coves, pristine islands, and the tranquility of Karelia's largest lake.

Where to Eat in Kainuu and Karelia

Embark on a gastronomic adventure through Kainuu and Karelia, where traditional flavors, locally sourced ingredients, and innovative culinary experiences await. From quaint cafés to fine dining establishments, explore the diverse and delectable dining scene these regions have to offer.

Kainuu

Kajaani Culinary Haven

Explore Kajaani's culinary landscape, where local restaurants blend traditional Finnish cuisine with international influences. Indulge in dishes crafted from locally sourced ingredients, showcasing the region's agricultural richness.

Must-Try Dish: Sample the Kainuun Rönttönen, a traditional pastry filled with barley porridge, lingonberry jam, and butter, providing a sweet and hearty treat.

Vuokatti Dining Experiences

In Vuokatti, restaurants take pride in creating menus inspired by the changing seasons. Enjoy dishes that reflect the bounties of nature, with a focus on fresh produce and locally caught fish.

Must-Try Dish: Muikku, a local delicacy featuring vendace, a small whitefish, typically served fried and enjoyed with a side of local potatoes.

Karelia

Joensuu's Culinary Scene

Joensuu's proximity to nature is reflected in its culinary offerings. Visit the bustling market square to discover a variety of fresh produce, local cheeses, and traditional Karelian pastries.

Must-Try Dish: A thin pastry filled with rice porridge or mashed potatoes, often served with egg butter, called Karjalanpiirakka.

Koli National Park Cuisine

Indulge in a unique dining experience with panoramic views of Koli National Park. Some restaurants in the area offer terrace dining, allowing you to savor local dishes while immersed in the breathtaking landscapes.

Must-Try Dish: Try the local game, like elk or reindeer, prepared with a modern twist, showcasing the culinary creativity inspired by the region's natural surroundings.

Address: Yla-Kolintie 1, 83960 Koli.

Shopping Guide

Uncover the hidden gems of Kainuu and Karelia with a shopping guide that leads you through local markets, artisan boutiques, and cultural hubs. From traditional crafts to contemporary designs, these regions offer a diverse array of shopping experiences, allowing you to bring home a piece of their unique charm.

Kainuu

Kajaani's Craft Boutiques

Explore Kajaani's craft boutiques, where local artisans showcase their handmade creations. These boutiques offer an authentic taste of Kainuu's artistic heritage, featuring traditional textiles and unique ceramics. Consider purchasing a "puukko," a traditional Finnish knife known for its craftsmanship and functional design.

Vuokatti Souvenirs

In Vuokatti, find souvenirs that celebrate the region's sporting legacy. Look for memorabilia from international sports events hosted in the area, including skiing and biathlon competitions. Grab a Vuokatti-themed hoodie or beanie, perfect for staying cozy during the colder months.

Karelia

Joensuu's Art Galleries

Wander through Joensuu's art galleries, where local artists showcase paintings, sculptures, and unique pieces inspired by Karelian landscapes. These galleries offer a glimpse into the vibrant artistic scene of the region. Consider purchasing a piece of "Karelian pottery," known for its intricate designs and rich cultural significance.

Koli National Park Souvenirs

Explore souvenir shops around Koli National Park, offering an array of nature-inspired keepsakes. Look for items adorned with images of the park's iconic landscapes, such as postcards, prints, and locally crafted ornaments. Take home a jar of local honey harvested from the blossoms of Koli's diverse flora.

Sports and Leisure Activities

Vuokatti Sports Center

Vuokatti in Sotkamo, a versatile year-round destination, is renowned for its outdoor pursuits. In winter, it transforms into a popular ski resort, while summer beckons with opportunities for hiking, golfing, and water sports by the shores of Lake Nuasjärvi. Visitors can unwind in saunas and pools and indulge in wellness treatments – making it the perfect retreat after a day of outdoor adventures.

Address: Opistontie 4, 88610 Vuokatti.

Did You Know?

Vuokatti has gained international recognition as a training ground for top athletes, hosting various sports competitions and providing state-of-the-art facilities.

Accommodations

Retreats in the North

Discover a range of accommodations in Kainuu and Karelia, each offering a unique blend of comfort and immersive experiences. From cozy lodges surrounded by nature to elegant hotels in cultural hubs, find the perfect place to unwind and make the most of your journey through these northern landscapes.

Kainuu

Horel Kajaani

Nestled in the woodlands near the Sipinen River, this retreat offers a tranquil escape with scenic views. Choose from cozy cabins or modern rooms in the main lodge. Enjoy riverside walks and the soothing ambiance of nature.

Address: Onnelantie 1, 87100 Kajaani.

Vuokatti Chalet Living

Experience the charm of chalet living in Vuokatti. Stay in well-appointed chalets with modern amenities and easy access to outdoor activities. Many chalets feature private saunas, allowing you to relax after a day of exploration.

Address: Opistontie 6, 88615 Vuokatti.

Karelia

Joensuu City Center Hotels

Explore Joensuu from the heart of the city with a stay in one of its centrally located hotels. Enjoy proximity to cultural attractions, vibrant markets, and local eateries. Ideal for those who wish to immerse themselves in city life.

Koli National Park Lodges

Choose from a selection of lodges around Koli National Park, offering breathtaking views of the surrounding landscapes. Some lodges provide terrace dining, allowing you to savor local dishes while taking in the beauty of Koli.

Choose your accommodations wisely to make the most of your journey through Kainuu and Karelia. Whether you prefer the tranquility of a riverside retreat, the urban charm of city center hotels, or the adventure of wilderness cabins, each option invites you to experience the unique character of these northern realms.

Chapter 7: Savo and Central Finland

Savo is located in the heart of Finland and is characterized by various stunning lakes, dense forests, and charming towns. Housing the largest lake in Finland, Lake Saimaa, the region's landscape is a must-visit for nature enthusiasts, offering chances for tranquil boat rides, hiking through ancient forests, and witnessing the vibrant Finnish wildlife. Savo is also rich in cultural heritage, with towns like Kuopio and Mikkeli showcasing a blend of modernity and tradition. Kuopio has a lively market square and the iconic Puijo Tower, from which you can enjoy the panoramic views of the surrounding lakes. Meanwhile, Mikkeli, situated by Lake Saimaa, has several historical landmarks to explore, including the Headquarters Museum with its ties to World War II. Savo is not just a destination; it's an immersive experience where natural beauty harmonizes with the echoes of Finnish traditions.

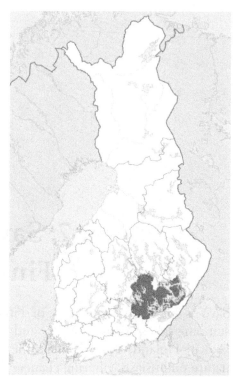

North Savo on the map.[50]   South Savo on the map.[51]

Likewise, Central Finland, with its diverse landscapes and vibrant urban centers, is a captivating region that seamlessly blends the tranquility of nature with modern urban amenities. The city of Jyväskylä, often hailed as the City of Light, is renowned for its architectural legacy, particularly the works of Alvar Aalto. Here, urban elegance meets the serenity of the surrounding lakes, creating a unique ambiance. The region's extensive network of lakes, including Päijänne and Keitele, has breathtaking scenery and various outdoor activities. Beyond the urban landscape, Saarijärvi and Keuruu add their own charm to Central Finland. Saarijärvi beckons with its pristine nature, including the Pyhä-Häkki National Park, while Keuruu, with its historical wooden architecture, invites visitors to stroll through the charming streets of Old Keuruu. Central Finland is not just a geographical expanse; it's an enchanting mosaic where the natural and urban elements coalesce, inviting travelers to immerse themselves in its beauty and cultural richness.

Brief Historical Background

The region of Savo and Central Finland, nestled in the heart of the country, boasts a rich historical tapestry that reflects Finnish culture. Historically, this area has played a significant role in Finland's development, contributing to its cultural heritage, economic vitality, and social fabric.

During the medieval period, Savo and Central Finland were characterized by the presence of numerous lakes and dense forests, shaping the lives of the local inhabitants. These natural features not only influenced the traditional ways of life but also served as vital transportation routes for trade and communication.

The region has witnessed the ebb and flow of various historical influences, including Swedish and Russian dominions. Under Swedish rule, Savo and Central Finland became part of the larger Kingdom of Sweden, and the cultural imprint of this era is still visible in local traditions and architecture. The area's affiliation with the Swedish Crown lasted until the early 19th century when Finland was ceded to Russia in 1809 following the Finnish War.

Under Russian rule, efforts to promote industrialization and modernization gained momentum. The construction of the Saimaa Canal in the late 19th century, linking Lake Saimaa to the Gulf of Finland, played a crucial role in enhancing transportation and trade in the region. The canal became a vital artery for the timber industry, connecting inland waterways to international markets.

In the early 20th century, as Finland gained its independence from Russia in 1917, Savo and Central Finland became integral to the nation-building process. The region contributed significantly to the evolving cultural identity of Finland, with its residents actively participating in the creation of a distinct Finnish ethos.

The charm of Savo and Central Finland lies not only in its historical significance but also in the preservation of local traditions, dialects, and architectural heritage. Today, the area attracts visitors with its blend of historical landmarks, picturesque landscapes, and a vibrant cultural scene that pays homage to its storied past. From the wooden architecture of Kuopio to the serene beauty of Lake Keitele, Savo and Central Finland invite exploration into a history shaped by nature, trade, and the resilience of its people.

Main Attractions

Kuopio

Puijo Tower

Puijo Tower.[52]

Perched atop Puijo Hill, the Puijo Tower is an iconic symbol of Kuopio. Offering breathtaking panoramic views of the city, lakes, and lush landscapes, reaching the top is a memorable experience accessible by a scenic road or a leisurely hike.

As of the writing of this book, the opening hours are Monday to Saturday from 10 am to 6 pm, and Sunday from 10 am to 4 pm. However, please make sure to double-check the hours online should there be any slight changes to their schedule.

Address: Puijontie, 135, 70300 Kuopio.

Did You Know?

Puijo Tower, besides being a scenic viewpoint, is also a hub for winter sports. During the snowy season, the Puijo Ski Jumping Hills nearby hosts international competitions, adding a touch of adrenaline to the serene landscape.

Lively Market Square

Kuopio's Market Square is a vibrant gathering place where locals and visitors alike engage in a lively atmosphere. Stroll through stalls filled with fresh produce and local crafts, immersing yourself in the daily life of Kuopio.

As of the writing of this book, you can visit the Market Square at any time during your trip. However, please double-check the opening hours online should there be any changes to their schedule.

Address: Kauppakatu 45, 70110 Kuopio.

Did You Know?

The market square is not just a daytime destination. In the summer evenings, it transforms into a cultural hotspot with live performances, creating a festive atmosphere for all to enjoy.

Kuopio Museum

Providing a comprehensive journey through the city's history, the Kuopio Museum features exhibits, artifacts, and interactive displays. Explore Kuopio's roots and modern evolution through engaging displays.

As of the writing of this book, the following are the opening hours of Kuopio Museum:

- Wednesday from 10 am to 7 pm.
- Thursday to Friday and Tuesday from 10 am to 5 pm.
- Closed on Monday.

However, please make sure to double-check the opening hours online should there be any slight changes to their schedule.

Address: Museokatu 1, 70100 Kuopio.

Did You Know?

Kuopio Museum has a unique exhibit showcasing the city's connection to the world of astronomy. The city's observatory has been contributing to astronomical research since the late 19th century.

Kalakukko Fish Pastries

A culinary highlight of Kuopio, Kalakukko is a traditional Finnish fish pastry. Savor the delicious combination of fish and pastry at local bakeries, adding a flavorful kick to your visit.

Did You Know?

Kalakukko is more than just a treat for the taste buds. It is also a symbol of local traditions. It has its roots in Eastern Finland, particularly in the Savo region, making it a culinary emblem of Kuopio's cultural heritage.

Savonlinna

Olavinlinna Castle

Olavinlinna Castle.[53]

Dominating the shores of Lake Saimaa, Olavinlinna Castle is a medieval fortress hosting the annual Savonlinna Opera Festival. Explore the castle's history and enjoy performances against the stunning backdrop of the lake.

As of the writing of this book, Olavinlinna Castle is open every day from 11 am to 6 pm. However, please make sure to double-check the opening hours online should there be any slight changes to their schedule.

Address: 57130 Savonlinna.

Did You Know?

Olavinlinna Castle has a mysterious past, with legends of ghosts and historical events. Some believe the castle is haunted, adding an extra layer of intrigue to its cultural significance.

Linnansaari National Park

Linnansaari National Park.[54]

Nature enthusiasts find solace in the pristine beauty of Linnansaari National Park. Accessible by boat, the park offers tranquility, hiking trails, and opportunities for birdwatching in the serene ambiance of Lake Saimaa.

As of the writing of this book, you can visit Linnansaari National Park at any time during your trip. However, please make sure to double-check the opening hours online should there be any slight changes to their schedules.

Address: Kiramontie 27, 58130 Oravi.

Did You Know?

Linnansaari is a haven for nature lovers and a sanctuary for the endangered Saimaa ringed seal. The park plays a crucial role in conservation efforts for this unique species.

Mikkeli

Headquarters Museum

Mikkeli's Headquarters Museum delves into the city's role during World War II, showcasing military history and wartime artifacts. Gain insights into Mikkeli's unique contributions to Finnish history.

As of the writing of this book, the opening hours are Monday to Saturday from 10 am to 5 pm and is closed on Sunday. However, please make sure to double-check the opening hours online should there be any slight changes to their schedule.

Address: Ristimaenkatu 4, 50100 Mikkeli.

Did You Know?

Mikkeli played a crucial role in the Continuation War, and the Headquarters Museum houses a collection of war memorabilia, providing a poignant look into the city's wartime experiences.

Mikkeli Cathedral

Mikkeli Cathedral.[55]

A neo-Gothic masterpiece, the Mikkeli Cathedral graces the city's skyline with elegant spires. Explore the cathedral's interiors adorned with stained glass windows, showcasing serene beauty against the backdrop of Lake Saimaa.

As of the writing of this book, the opening hours are Monday to Saturday from 11 am to 6 pm and Sunday from 10 am to 5 pm. However, please make sure to double-check the opening hours online should there be any slight changes to their schedule.

Address: Ristimaenkatu 2, 50100 Mikkeli.

Did You Know?

The Mikkeli Cathedral is not just a place of worship. It has also served as a backdrop for various cultural events and concerts, blending spirituality with artistic expression.

Astuvansalmi Rock Paintings

Astuvansalmi Rock Paintings.[56]

Venture to Ristiina to witness the ancient Astuvansalmi rock paintings, providing a fascinating glimpse into the lives of the area's earliest inhabitants. These prehistoric artworks add a layer of historical richness to Mikkeli's cultural tapestry.

As of the writing of this book, you can visit the Astuvansalmi rock paintings at any time during your trip. However, please make sure to double-check the opening hours online should there be any slight changes to their schedule.

Address: Mikkeli, Suurlahdentie 2039, 52360 Someenjarvi.

Did You Know?

The Astuvansalmi rock paintings form one of the largest prehistoric rock art sites in Finland, offering a window into the rituals and expressions of ancient communities.

Mikkeli Music Festival

Set against the city's tranquil landscapes, the annual Mikkeli Music Festival brings classical music to the forefront. Enjoy performances by renowned musicians, blending harmonious melodies with the serene beauty of Mikkeli's natural surroundings.

Did You Know?

The Mikkeli Music Festival has become a cultural cornerstone, attracting both local and international artists. It's not just an auditory experience but also a celebration of Mikkeli's commitment to the arts.

Varkaus

Mekaanisen Musiikin Museo (Mechanical Music Museum)

Mekaanisen Musiikin Museo.[57]

Varkaus beckons with the Mekaanisen Musiikin Museo, where the Mechanical Music Museum offers a captivating exploration of industrial history. Discover a unique collection of mechanical musical instruments showcasing the intersection of technology and artistry.

As of the writing of this book, the opening hours are Tuesday to Sunday from 12 pm to 5 pm and closed on Monday. However, please make sure to double-check the opening hours online should there be any slight changes to their schedule.

Address: Pelimanninkatu 8, 78250 Varkaus.

Did You Know?

Varkaus has a robust industrial legacy, and the Mechanical Music Museum's collection includes rare and unique pieces, providing a glimpse into the city's mechanical innovations.

Varkaus Art Museum

Immerse yourself in the cultural richness of Varkaus at the Varkaus Art Museum. Featuring diverse artworks by local and international artists, the museum highlights the city's commitment to artistic expression, making it a must-visit for art enthusiasts.

As of the writing of this book, the opening hours are:

- Wednesday and Friday from 9 am to 4 pm.
- Thursday from 9 am to 8 pm.
- Saturday from 10 am to 5 pm.
- Closed on Monday and Tuesday.

However, please make sure to double-check the opening hours online should there be any slight changes to their schedule.

Address: Satakunnankatu 1, 78300 Varkaus.

Did You Know?

The Varkaus Art Museum actively promotes contemporary art, showcasing the city's evolving cultural landscape and contributing to the dialogue of modern artistic expression.

Central Finland

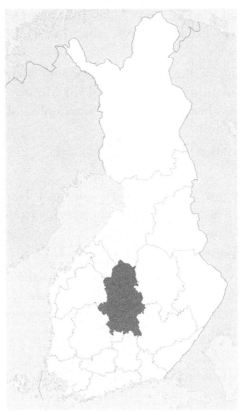

Central Finland on the map.[58]

Jyväskylä

Alvar Aalto Museum

Alvar Aalto Museum.[59]

Jyväskylä, renowned as the city of Alvar Aalto, pays homage to the iconic Finnish architect at the Alvar Aalto Museum. Delve into Aalto's life and works through exhibits, showcasing his influence on modern architecture and design.

As of the writing of this book, the opening hours are Tuesday to Sunday from 11 am to 6 pm and closed on Monday. However, please make sure to double-check the opening hours online should there be any changes to their schedule.

Address: Alvar Aallon katu 7, 40600 Jyväskylä.

Did You Know?

Jyväskylä is not just a museum; it's a living tribute to Alvar Aalto's legacy. The city itself is adorned with Aalto's architectural marvels, creating a dynamic urban canvas.

Jyväskylä Arts Festival

The annual Jyväskylä Arts Festival infuses the city with cultural dynamism. Attendees can enjoy a diverse range of performances, exhibitions, and events, creating a vibrant atmosphere that celebrates Jyväskylä's artistic spirit.

Did You Know?

The Jyväskylä Arts Festival is not confined to traditional venues. Street performances and art installations pop up throughout the city, turning Jyväskylä into a dynamic and interactive cultural playground.

Lakeside Trails

Jyväskylä's surrounding lakes provide enchanting trails for nature lovers. Whether walking, cycling, or simply enjoying the lakeside tranquility, these trails offer a scenic retreat and opportunities for water sports amid the region's natural beauty.

Did You Know?

Jyväskylä's lakeside trails are not just for outdoor enthusiasts. They also serve as venues for various events, including open-air concerts and cultural happenings, seamlessly blending nature with cultural experiences.

Saarijärvi
Pyhä-Häkki National Park

Pyhä-Häkki National Park.[60]

Saarijärvi offers a genuine natural retreat with the Pyhä-Häkki National Park. Ancient forests, pristine lakes, and diverse flora and fauna create an immersive experience for those seeking solace in nature.

As of the writing of this book, you can visit the Pyhä-Häkki National Park at any time during your trip. However, please make sure to double-check the opening hours online should there be any slight changes to their schedule.

Address: 43170 Saarijärvi.

Did You Know?

Pyhä-Häkki National Park is also a sanctuary for Finland's oldest trees. Some of the trees in the park are over 500 years old, adding a sense of awe to the natural surroundings.

Lake Saarijärvi

Lake Saarijärvi.[61]

The stunning Lake Saarijärvi provides a perfect setting for boating and fishing, allowing visitors to unwind amidst the tranquil beauty of nature. Whether on the water or along the shores, Lake Saarijärvi invites exploration and relaxation.

As of the writing of this book, you can visit Lake Saarijärvi at any time during your trip. However, please make sure to double-check the opening hours online should there be any slight changes to their schedule.

Did You Know?

Lake Saarijärvi is not just a serene backdrop. It's also a site for various water-based events and festivals, turning the lake into a dynamic cultural space.

Keuruu

Old Keuruu

Step into the past with a visit to Old Keuruu, where historical wooden architecture preserves the essence of bygone eras. Stroll through charming streets, surrounded by well-preserved buildings that tell tales of Keuruu's rich heritage.

As of the writing of this book, you can visit Old Keuruu at any time during your trip. However, please make sure to double-check the opening hours online should there be any slight changes to their schedule.

Address: Kangasmannilantie 2-4, 42700 Keuruu.

Did You Know?

Old Keuruu is more than just a historical district. It's also a living community. Some of the buildings are still in use, providing a glimpse into the continuity of Keuruu's architectural legacy.

Keuruu Museum

Keuruu Museum.[62]

Delve into the cultural gems of Keuruu at the Keuruu Museum. Exhibits showcase artifacts and historical items that narrate the city's history, providing a comprehensive understanding of Keuruu's evolution over the years.

As of the writing of this book, the opening hours are Tuesday to Saturday from 11 am to 4 pm and closed on Sunday and Monday. However, please make sure to double-check the opening hours online should there be any slight changes to their schedule.

Address: Kangasmannilantie 4, 42700 Keuruu.

Did You Know?

The Keuruu Museum actively involves the community in preserving local heritage. Residents contribute personal stories and items, creating a dynamic and inclusive cultural narrative.

Pihlajavesi Wilderness Church

Pihlajavesi Wilderness Church.[63]

The Pihlajavesi Wilderness Church stands as a cultural and architectural landmark. Nestled amidst pristine lakes and forests, the church offers a peaceful retreat, allowing visitors to connect with nature and experience the serenity of Keuruu's surroundings.

As of the writing of this book, you can visit the Pihlajavesi Wilderness Church at any time during your trip. However, please make sure to double-check the opening hours online should there be any slight changes to their schedule.

Address: Eramaakirkontie 221, 42910 Pihlajavesi.

Did You Know?

The Pihlajavesi Wilderness Church is also a venue for cultural events, including concerts and exhibitions, adding a cultural dimension to its serene setting.

Did You Know?

Keuruu's natural surroundings, including pristine lakes and forests, provide an ideal backdrop for outdoor activities such as hiking and camping, allowing visitors to connect with nature and fully immerse themselves in the region's tranquility.

Transport in Savo and Central Finland

Public Transportation

Savo: The cities in Savo, including Kuopio and Mikkeli, have well-established public transportation systems. Buses are a popular mode of travel, providing convenient access to various neighborhoods and attractions.

Central Finland: In cities like Jyväskylä, public transportation is efficient, with an extensive bus network connecting the city and its surrounding areas. Trains are also available, connecting Jyväskylä with other major cities in Finland.

Car Rentals

Savo: Renting a car in Savo, particularly in cities like Kuopio, offers flexibility and convenience. It's an excellent option for exploring picturesque landscapes and reaching more remote attractions.

Central Finland: Car rental services are readily available in Central Finland, allowing visitors to explore the region at their own pace. This is especially beneficial for accessing natural parks and lakeside areas.

Train Services

Savo: Savo is well-connected by train services, with Kuopio and Mikkeli serving as key railway hubs. Trains provide a comfortable and scenic way to travel between cities and enjoy the Finnish countryside.

Central Finland: Jyväskylä, in Central Finland, is a major railway junction offering efficient train connections to various parts of the country. Train travel is a popular choice for those exploring the region.

Cycling

Savo: Both Kuopio and Mikkeli have embraced cycling as a mode of transportation. Bike rentals and dedicated cycling lanes make it easy for visitors to explore the cities and their surroundings on two wheels.

Central Finland: Jyväskylä is known for its bike-friendly infrastructure, encouraging locals and visitors to use bicycles for commuting and leisure. Cycling is an excellent way to enjoy the city's lakeside trails.

Air Travel

Savo: Savo has airports, such as Kuopio Airport, providing domestic flights. Air travel is convenient for those looking to explore Savo and its neighboring regions.

Central Finland: Jyväskylä Airport caters to domestic flights, offering quick access to Central Finland. This is particularly useful for those arriving from other parts of Finland.

Boat Services

Savo: Given the region's numerous lakes, boat services are available in certain areas, offering scenic cruises and transportation between lakeside destinations.

Central Finland: With its lakeside setting, Jyväskylä also provides boat services, allowing travelers to enjoy the breathtaking landscapes from a different perspective.

Navigating Savo and Central Finland is made convenient through a well-connected transportation system, offering various options for exploring the cities, natural wonders, and cultural attractions in these Finnish regions.

Experiences in Savo and Central Finland

Finnish Lakeland Cruises

Savo: Explore the scenic lakes of Savo, including Lake Saimaa, on a leisurely cruise. Enjoy the tranquility of the water, picturesque landscapes, and, in some areas, historic steamship journeys.

Central Finland: Cruise along the beautiful lakes near Jyväskylä for a relaxing experience. Some cruises offer themed tours, providing insights into the region's nature and culture.

Savo Food Tours

Savo: Embark on a culinary journey through Savo's local flavors. Participate in food tours in cities like Kuopio, where you can savor traditional Finnish dishes and explore bustling food markets.

Central Finland: Jyväskylä offers food-focused experiences, with guided tours showcasing the region's culinary delights. Discover local specialties and immerse yourself in the vibrant food scene.

Cultural Festivals

Savo: Savo hosts various cultural festivals throughout the year. Attend events like the Kuopio Dance Festival, where you can experience the rich cultural tapestry through dance performances.

Central Finland: Immerse yourself in the cultural vibrancy of Jyväskylä with events like the Jyväskylä Arts Festival. Enjoy performances, exhibitions, and artistic expressions that highlight the city's dynamic cultural scene.

Sauna Experiences

Savo: Experience the traditional Finnish sauna culture in Savo. Some accommodations offer private saunas, providing a relaxing and authentic way to unwind.

Central Finland: Jyväskylä is known for its sauna culture. Visit public saunas or lakeside saunas for a truly Finnish experience, combining relaxation with breathtaking natural surroundings.

Did You Know?

The summer months bring forth unique experiences, such as the Midnight Sun events. Participate in Midnight Sun cruises or festivals in both regions, celebrating the magical phenomenon of extended daylight hours.

Where to Eat in Savo and Central Finland

Name	Information	Address
Ristorante Momento Matkus (Kuopio)	Located in Matkus Shopping Center, Ristorante Momento Matkus offers a delightful dining experience. Enjoy Italian cuisine prepared with fresh, local ingredients.	Matkuksentie 60, 70800 Kuopio
Muikkuravintola Sampo (Kuopio)	Embrace the ambiance of a historic building at Muikkuravintola Sampo. This restaurant in Kuopio's market square serves traditional Finnish dishes, including local specialties like Kalakukko.	Kauppakatu 13, 70100 Kuopio

Fernando's Restaurant (Mikkeli)	Fernando's Restaurant offers delicious meals from international cuisines, including American and Italian, made with fresh, locally-produced ingredients.	Maaherrankatu 17, 50100 Mikkeli
Ravintola Vaiha (Mikkeli)	This Mikkeli restaurant focuses on locally sourced ingredients, providing a taste of authentic Finnish cuisine as well as international cuisines. The restaurant also serves a wide variety of wines, beers, and ciders.	Mannerheimintie 1, 50100 Mikkeli
Savutuvan Apaja (Jyväskylä)	Explore the flavors of Finnish smokehouse cuisine at Savutuvan Apaja. Situated by Lake Jyväsjärvi, this restaurant offers a unique blend of traditional dishes with a modern twist.	Opinsaunankiuas 1, 40820 Jyväskylä
Harmooni (Jyväskylä)	For a fine dining experience, visit Harmooni in the heart of Jyväskylä. The restaurant's diverse menu features carefully crafted dishes using local and seasonal ingredients.	Vainonkatu 12, Hannikaisen 39, 40100 Jyväskylä

Frisee Saarijärvi (Saarijärvi)	Enjoy a cozy atmosphere Frisee Saarijärvi. This café serves delightful pastries, cakes, and light meals, making it an ideal spot for a relaxing break.	Kauppakatu 1, 43100 Saarijärvi
Wanha Mestari Mannila (Saarijärvi)	Located near the center of Saarijärvi, Wanha Mestari Mannila offers delicious food and great music. Sample their menu with a variety of dishes, combining local flavors and international influences.	Kauppakatu 4, 43100 Saarijärvi
Nyyssis (Keuruu)	This restaurant offers a tasty selection of dishes, including pizzas, burgers, and more delicacies and is located on a campsite near Lake Keurusselkä.	Nyyssanniementie 104, 42700 Keuruu
IltaLenkki (Keuruu)	This restaurant offers delicious grilled meals and Finnish dishes with a cozy atmosphere.	Koulutie 7, 42700 Keuruu

Did You Know?

Many restaurants in the region emphasize the use of local and seasonal ingredients. The culinary scene is shaped by the proximity to nature, ensuring fresh and high-quality flavors in each dish.

Discover the culinary delights of Savo and Central Finland by exploring these recommended eateries. Whether you prefer lakeside views, historic settings, or farm-to-table experiences, the region offers a diverse range of dining options to suit every palate.

Shopping Guide

Kuopio

Kuopion Kauppahalli: Dive into Kuopio's vibrant food culture at Kuopion Kauppahalli, the city's historic market hall. Discover local produce, artisanal goods, and traditional Finnish delicacies.

Address: Kauppakatu 45, 70110 Kuopio.

Kauppakatu: Explore Kauppakatu, Kuopio's main shopping street. Here, you'll find a mix of boutiques, fashion stores, and specialty shops offering everything from clothing to unique Finnish design.

Mikkeli

Mikkeli Market Square: Dive into the heart of Mikkeli's shopping scene at the Market Square. Find local handicrafts, fresh produce, and authentic Finnish goods.

Address: Hallituskatu 3, 50100 Mikkeli.

Jyväskylä

Jyväskylä Market Square: Stroll through Jyväskylä Market Square, a bustling hub for fresh produce, local crafts, and a vibrant atmosphere. Discover handmade souvenirs and gifts from regional artisans.

Saarijärvi

Saarijärvi Craft Shops: Saarijärvi is home to charming craft shops where you can find handmade textiles, pottery, and other artisanal items. Support local artists and take home one-of-a-kind treasures.

Antique Shops: Explore Saarijärvi's antique shops for a journey into the past. Discover unique vintage finds, including furniture, decor items, and collectibles.

Keuruu

Old Keuruu Boutiques: Wander through the boutiques of Old Keuruu, where you'll find shops housed in historic buildings. Browse for souvenirs, local crafts, and antiques.

Did You Know?

The region is known for its traditional crafts, including items made from birch bark, reindeer leather, and ceramics. Look for these unique crafts as authentic mementos of your visit.

Enjoy the local shopping scene of Savo and Central Finland, where market squares, boutiques, and craft shops offer a diverse array of goods.

Whether you're seeking traditional Finnish products, handmade crafts, or vintage treasures, these regions provide a delightful shopping experience.

Accommodations in Savo and Central Finland

Name	Information	Address
Scandic Kuopio (Kuopio)	Enjoy modern comforts at Scandic Kuopio, located near Lake Kallavesi. This hotel offers scenic views, wellness facilities, and easy access to Kuopio's attractions.	Satamakatu 1, 70100 Kuopio
Original Sokos Hotel Puijonsarvi (Kuopio)	Immerse yourself in the heart of Kuopio at Original Sokos Hotel Puijonsarvi. With its central location, comfortable rooms, and on-site dining options, it's a convenient choice for exploring the city.	Minna Canthin katu 16, 70100 Kuopio
Scandic Mikkeli (Mikkeli)	Experience tranquility and comfort at Scandic Mikkeli, a hotel near the central of Mikkeli. The hotel offers spacious rooms, a pool, a sauna, and a relaxing stay near attractions including the Mikkeli Cathedral.	Mikonkatu 9, 50100 Mikkeli

Sokos Hotel Vaakuna Mikkeli (Mikkeli)	Stay in the heart of Mikkeli at Sokos Hotel Vaakuna. This stylish hotel provides a central base for exploring the city, with modern amenities and comfortable accommodations.	Porrassalmenkatu 9, 50100 Mikkeli
Solo Sokos Hotel Paviljonki (Jyväskylä)	Indulge in urban elegance at Solo Sokos Hotel Paviljonki in Jyväskylä. Located by Lake Jyväsjärvi, the hotel offers contemporary design, exquisite dining, and scenic views.	Lutakonaukio 10, 40100 Jyväskylä
Scandic Jyväskylä City (Jyväskylä)	Choose Scandic Jyväskylä City for a comfortable stay near the city center. With its convenient location, wellness amenities, and modern rooms, it caters to both business and leisure travelers.	Vainonkatu 3, 40100 Jyväskylä
Saarijärvi Hotel Ruustinna (Saarijärvi)	Set in a charming manor, Saarijärvi Hotel Ruustinna offers wonderful rooms surrounded by nature that provide a historical atmosphere. This is also	Paavontie 1, 43100 Saarijärvi

	a restaurant below serving authentic Finnish dishes.	
Hotelli Keurusselkä (Keuruu)	Enjoy lakeside serenity at Hotelli Keurusselkä in Keuruu. This hotel provides comfortable accommodations, lakeside views, and proximity to outdoor activities.	Keurusselantie 134, 42700 Keuruu
Hostelli Nonna (Keuruu)	Stay at Hostelli Nonna to be close to the center of Keuruu while sticking to your budget. This hostel offers comfortable apartments and rooms with all the appliances you may need during your stay.	Kiveläntie 17 B 10 42700, 42700 Keuruu

Did You Know?

Both Savo and Central Finland: Many accommodations in the region emphasize sustainability and eco-friendly practices. Look for hotels and lodges that prioritize environmental responsibility for a more nature-conscious stay.

Discover a range of accommodations in Savo and Central Finland, from lakeside retreats to urban hotels and historical guesthouses. Whether you seek serene nature escapes or convenient city stays, these regions offer a variety of options to suit different preferences and travel styles.

Chapter 8: Ostrobothnia, Seinäjoki, Kokkola, Oulu, and Raahe

Located in the western part of Finland, Ostrobothnia, or Pohjanmaa in Finnish, is a region popular for its captivating landscapes, vibrant cultural heritage, and a unique mix of modernism and traditionalism. The coastal region of Ostrobothnia connects to the sea, harbors diverse communities, and has a rich history, making it an intriguing destination for travelers seeking an authentic Finnish experience.

Ostrobothnia on the map.[64]

Brief Historical Background

Ostrobothnia has a fascinating history that depicts Finland's development as a nation. The region has been inhabited for thousands of years, with evidence of ancient settlements dating back to the Stone Age. Over the centuries, Ostrobothnia has housed various cultures, from the Vikings to the Swedish and Russian empires.

It was the Swedish who were keen to develop the region. During the Middle Ages, Ostrobothnia became a part of the Kingdom of Sweden, and this Swedish influence can still be seen in the region's architecture, traditions, and even language. The rule under the Swedish empire has left its mark, which you'll find in charming wooden buildings, medieval churches, and a cultural identity as a testament to this shared history.

In the 18th century, the people of Ostrobothnia achieved significant agricultural feats, making the fertile plains to be known as the breadbasket of Finland. The vast expanses of fields and farmlands contribute to the landscape and the region's agrarian identity.

The 19th and 20th centuries brought about industrialization, transforming Ostrobothnia into a hub of commerce and trade. The bustling coastal towns became centers of maritime activity, and the region's economy diversified with the growth of manufacturing and services. Ostrobothnia also played a role in the Finnish Civil War (1918) and the Winter War (1939-1940), events further shaping the region's history and resilience.

Today, Ostrobothnia stands as a testament to the harmonious coexistence of tradition and modernity. Visitors can explore its historical sites, engage with the warm and welcoming local communities, and witness the ongoing evolution of this vibrant region on the western coast of Finland.

Main Attractions

Kvarken Archipelago (UNESCO World Heritage Site): Vaasa's proximity to the Kvarken Archipelago offers a chance to explore unique geological landscapes and witness diverse wildlife. The shifting terrain due to post-glacial rebound is a fascinating natural phenomenon.

As of the writing of this book, you can visit the Kvarken Archipelago at any time during your visit. However, please make sure to double-check the opening hours online should there be any slight changes to their schedule.

Vaasa Maritime Museum: Unveiling the maritime heritage of the region, this museum showcases the importance of seafaring in Vaasa's history, including shipbuilding and trading traditions.

As of the writing of this book, the opening hours are Monday to Friday from 11:30 am to 6 pm and closed on Saturday and Sunday. However, please make sure to double-check the opening hours online should there be any slight changes to their schedule.

Address: Salmikatu 27, 65200 Vaasa.

Vaasa Maritime Museum.[65]

Did You Know?

Vaasa is not only recognized for its sustainable practices but also for being a bilingual city, with both Finnish and Swedish being official languages. This bilingualism reflects the historical ties between Finland and Sweden in the region.

Seinäjoki

Seinäjoki on the map.[66]

Lakeuden Risti (Cross of the Plains): Designed by Alvar Aalto, this cross-shaped church is an architectural gem and a symbol of Seinäjoki. It is part of the city's administrative and cultural center.

As of the writing of this book, the opening hours are every day from 3 pm to 5 pm. However, please make sure to double-check the opening hours online should there be any slight changes to their schedules.

Address: Koulukatu 24, 60100 Seinäjoki.

Lakeuden Risti.[67]

Provinssi Rock and Tango Festivals: Seinäjoki comes alive with these annual music festivals, attracting music enthusiasts from around the country. The festivals celebrate diverse genres, from rock to tango, showcasing Finland's rich musical culture.

Törnävä Museum Area: Offering a glimpse into traditional Ostrobothnian life, this museum area features historic buildings and exhibits that highlight the cultural heritage of the region.

Address: Törnäväntie 23, Seinäjoki.

Did You Know?

Seinäjoki is often referred to as the "City of Southern Ostrobothnia," emphasizing its regional significance and influence.

Kokkola

Kokkola on the map.[68]

Neristan (Old Town): Kokkola's Old Town boasts well-preserved wooden houses, creating a charming atmosphere. Neristan is a testament to the city's medieval roots and architectural heritage.

K.H. Renlund Museum - Provincial Museum of Central Ostrobothnia: Focusing on maritime history, this museum showcases Kokkola's seafaring traditions, including exhibits on shipbuilding and navigation.

As of the writing of this book, the opening hours are Tuesday, Wednesday and Friday to Sunday from 11 am to 4 pm, Thursday from 11 am to 6 pm, and closed on Monday. However, please make sure to double-check the opening hours online should there be any slight changes to their schedule.

Address: Pitkansillankatu 39, 67100 Kokkola.

K.H. Renlund Museum.[69]

Tankar Island: A serene retreat for nature lovers featuring a lighthouse, a seal hunter's hut, and a small herd of reindeer. The island provides a tranquil escape with its scenic beauty.

As of the writing this book, you can visit Tankar Island at any time during your trip.

Did You Know?

Kokkola's Venetian Night festival, with its boat parade and fireworks, is a spectacular event that brings the community together and showcases the city's lively cultural scene.

Oulu

Oulu on the map.[70]

Science Centre Tietomaa: Explore the wonders of science and technology in this interactive museum, highlighting Oulu's role as a technological hub. It's an engaging experience for visitors of all ages.

As of the writing of this book, Science Centre Tietomaa is currently closed for renovations and is expected to reopen in the summer of 2026.

Address: Nahkatehtaankatu 6, 90130 Oulu.

Nallikari Beach: A beautiful sandy beach near the city center, offering a relaxing escape. The beach is popular for various outdoor activities and events, especially during the summer months.

As of the writing of this book, you can visit Nallikari Beach at any time during your visit. However, please make sure to double check the opening hours online should there be any slight changes in their schedule.

Nallikari Beach.[71]

Oulu Music Video Festival: An annual event that celebrates the art of music videos, adding a dynamic cultural element to the city. It attracts music and film enthusiasts from across the region.

Did You Know?

Oulu is recognized for its vibrant startup ecosystem and technological innovations, making it a significant player in Finland's tech industry.

Raahe

Raahe on the map.[72]

Raahe Old Town: Known for its well-preserved wooden houses, the Old Town provides a glimpse into Raahe's maritime history and its significance as a trading port.

You can visit Raahe Old Town at any time during your trip.

Raahe Museum: Home to the world's oldest surviving diving suit, this museum delves into the maritime heritage of Raahe and showcases artifacts from different periods.

As of the writing of this book, the Raahe Museum is open Tuesday to Friday from 1 pm to 5 pm, Saturday from 12 pm to 4 pm, and closed on Sunday and Monday. However, please make sure to double-check the opening hours online should there be any slight changes in their schedule.

Raahe Museum.[73]

Raahe Jazz on the Beach Festival: Combining scenic coastal beauty with soulful music, this annual festival creates a unique and memorable experience for attendees.

Did You Know?

Raahe's archipelago adds a touch of magic to the town, offering visitors a chance to explore the enchanting coastal landscapes and experience the tranquility of the Baltic Sea.

Transportation

Ostrobothnia, with its diverse cities and picturesque landscapes, is well-connected by various modes of transportation, offering convenient options for travelers to explore the region.

Air Travel

Vaasa Airport: Serving as a major gateway to the region, Vaasa Airport connects Ostrobothnia to domestic and international destinations. Airlines provide regular flights, ensuring accessibility for both business and leisure travelers.

Kokkola-Pietarsaari Airport: Located in Kronoby, this airport facilitates air travel to and from Central Ostrobothnia, providing a convenient option for those exploring the region.

Oulu Airport: As a major hub in North Ostrobothnia, Oulu Airport offers extensive domestic and international flights, connecting the region to various destinations around the world.

Rail Transportation

The rail network in Ostrobothnia is well-developed, providing efficient connections between cities and neighboring regions. Visitors can enjoy scenic train journeys while experiencing the comfort of modern rail services.

Major railway stations include Vaasa Railway Station, Seinäjoki Railway Station, Kokkola Railway Station, and Oulu Railway Station. These stations are integral parts of the national rail network, offering regular services to other parts of Finland.

Road Travel

The road network in Ostrobothnia is extensive, making road travel a popular choice for both local commuters and tourists. Well-maintained highways and roads connect cities and rural areas, providing a convenient means of transportation.

Car rentals are available in major cities, offering flexibility for travelers to explore the region at their own pace. The road system was designed for easy navigation, allowing visitors to access attractions, nature reserves, and cultural sites easily.

Public Transportation

Cities like Vaasa, Seinäjoki, Kokkola, and Oulu have efficient public transportation systems, including buses. These systems are not only convenient for local commuting but also provide visitors with an accessible means of exploring urban areas and their attractions.

Additionally, taxi services are readily available in urban centers, offering a comfortable and flexible mode of transportation for those who prefer a personalized travel experience.

Maritime Travel

Given Ostrobothnia's coastal location, maritime travel is an integral part of the region's transportation infrastructure. Ferry services connect various islands, providing scenic journeys and access to unique archipelagos.

Ports like Vaasa Port and Kokkola Port play crucial roles in facilitating maritime transport, serving as hubs for cargo shipments and passenger ferries.

Did You Know?

Ostrobothnia's emphasis on sustainable development extends to its transportation sector. The region actively promotes eco-friendly initiatives, including the use of electric buses, bike-sharing programs, and a commitment to reduce carbon emissions in both urban and rural transport systems. Travelers can explore the region with the knowledge that efforts are being made to create a more sustainable and environmentally conscious transportation network.

Experiences

Ostrobothnia beckons travelers with a tapestry of experiences, blending cultural richness, natural wonders, and vibrant events. Whether you seek historical insights, musical rhythms, or immersive landscapes, Ostrobothnia offers a variety of thematic experiences.

Cultural Exploration

Vaasa Choir Festival: Immerse yourself in the harmonious ambiance of the Vaasa Choir Festival, an annual celebration of choral music that echoes through the streets.

Tango and Provinssi Rock Festivals (Seinäjoki): Let the rhythm take over at Seinäjoki's festivals. Dance to the iconic Finnish tango or rock out to diverse music genres in a lively festival setting.

Neristan (Kokkola Old Town): Wander through the cobblestone streets of Neristan in Kokkola, where well-preserved wooden houses tell tales of bygone eras, providing a charming cultural experience.

Nature and Adventure

Kvarken Archipelago: Explore the unique geological formations of the Kvarken Archipelago in Vaasa, a UNESCO World Heritage Site. Guided tours and boat trips reveal the fascinating landscapes shaped by post-glacial rebound.

Tankar Island (Kokkola): Seek tranquility on Tankar Island in Kokkola, featuring a lighthouse, a seal hunter's hut, and encounters with a small herd of reindeer—a peaceful retreat for nature enthusiasts.

Raahe Archipelago and Jazz on the Beach Festival: Immerse yourself in the coastal beauty of Raahe. Explore the picturesque archipelago and join the annual Jazz on the Beach festival, where music harmonizes with the stunning seaside backdrop.

Historical Exploration

Alvar Aalto's Architectural Marvels (Seinäjoki): Admire the architectural brilliance of Alvar Aalto in Seinäjoki, particularly the Lakeuden Risti (Cross of the Plains) church and the administrative and cultural center. Guided tours offer insights into Aalto's vision.

Raahe Museum: Step into the maritime history of Raahe at the Raahe Museum, home to the world's oldest surviving diving suit. Explore exhibits that showcase the town's seafaring traditions and its significance as a trading port.

Festivals and Events

Vaasa Wildlife Festival: Nature enthusiasts can revel in the Vaasa Wildlife Festival, celebrating the rich biodiversity of the region with guided tours, wildlife photography exhibitions, and interactive programs.

Venetian Night Festival (Kokkola): Join the lively atmosphere of Kokkola during the Venetian Night Festival. The boat parade, fireworks, and cultural events create a vibrant and unforgettable experience.

Oulu Music Video Festival: Experience the fusion of music and visual art at the Oulu Music Video Festival. Showcasing innovative music videos, this event adds a dynamic cultural element to the city's lively scene.

Did You Know?

Ostrobothnia's commitment to cultural diversity is reflected in its numerous festivals, showcasing everything from traditional Finnish tango to international choir performances. The region's events calendar ensures that visitors can immerse themselves in the rich tapestry of Ostrobothnian culture throughout the year.

Where to Eat

Explore Ostrobothnia's culinary landscape, where traditional Finnish flavors meet modern gastronomy. The region boasts a diverse array of restaurants and cafes, each offering a unique dining experience. From seaside views to historic settings, here are some noteworthy places to savor the tastes of Ostrobothnia.

Name	Information	Address
Bock's Corner Brewery (Vaasa)	Discover a cozy pub atmosphere at Bock's Corner Brewery, celebrated for its craft beers and hearty pub fare. Locally brewed beers and a welcoming ambiance make it a favored spot among locals and visitors alike.	Gerbyntie 16, 65230 Vaasa
Restaurant Strampen (Vaasa)	Enjoy seafood dishes with a scenic sea view at Restaurant Strampen. This establishment's menu emphasizes fresh catches and local ingredients, creating a memorable dining experience along the waterfront.	Rantakatu 7v. 65100 Vaasa

Holy Smoke (Seinäjoki)	Immerse yourself in food made using a charcoal grill at Holy Smoke. With a focus on burgers and steaks, this rustic restaurant offers delicious food and a great experience.	Koulukatu 20, 60100 Seinäjoki
Amarillo (Seinäjoki)	Satisfy Tex-Mex cravings at Amarillo in Seinäjoki. Vibrant surroundings and flavorful dishes, including sizzling fajitas and nachos, create a lively dining experience with an international touch.	Kauppatori 3, 60100 Seinäjoki
Kung's Kitchen (Kokkola)	Enjoy Asian Fusions dishes with a modern twist at Kung's Kitchen. Located near the center of Kokkola, this restaurant offers a taste of Asian cuisine with fresh, high-quality ingredients.	Pitkansillankatu 23, 67100 Kokkola
Café Kahvipuu (Kokkola)	Enjoy a cup of coffee at Café Kahvipuu, a classic cafe in Kokkola. Known for its friendly ambiance and selection of cakes and pastries, it provides a leisurely setting for a coffee break.	Isokatu 11, 67100 Kokkola

Ravintola Nallikari (Oulu)	Indulge in seaside dining at Ravintola Nallikari, offering panoramic views of the Gulf of Bothnia. The menu features a mix of local and international dishes, with a particular focus on delectable seafood.	Nallikarinranta 15, 90510 Oulu
Ravintola Puistola (Oulu)	Experience Nordic cuisine in this restaurant, where the menu is inspired by seasonal and locally sourced ingredients. The restaurant's elegant interior adds to the overall dining experience.	Pakkahuoneenkatu 15, 90100 Oulu
Pannukakkutalo (Oulu)	Treat yourself to Finnish pancakes with various toppings at Pannukakkutalo. This unique spot specializes in pancakes, offering a cozy atmosphere and a delightful menu.	Vattukuja 1, 90460 Oulu
Langin Kauppahuone (Raahe)	Step into the historic ambiance of Langin Kauppahuone and enjoy exceptional dishes. The restaurant's warm atmosphere and hearty menu showcase the region's culinary heritage	Kirkkokatu 19, 92100 Raahe

Raahen Fish and Café (Raahe)	Relish in the taste of freshly-cooked fish, Raahen Fish and Café offers authentic Finnish fish dishes and a variety of pastries. This café has wonderfully decorated indoor and outdoor areas.	Kirkkokatu 22 L 1, 92100 Raahe

Did You Know?

Ostrobothnia's commitment to sustainability extends to its culinary scene, with many restaurants emphasizing the use of locally sourced ingredients. Dining in the region not only offers delicious meals but also supports local farms and producers.

Shopping Guide

Ostrobothnia offers a unique shopping experience, blending local craftsmanship, Nordic design, and a touch of maritime flair. From traditional markets to modern boutiques, explore the region's shopping scene for distinctive items and souvenirs.

Vaasa

Vaasa Market Square: Begin your shopping adventure at Vaasa Market Square, where local vendors showcase fresh produce, artisanal goods, and traditional Finnish treats. This bustling market is an excellent place to immerse yourself in the local culture.

Address: Vaasan Kauppatori, 65100 Vaasa.

Rewell Center: For a mix of fashion, lifestyle, and dining, head to the Rewell Center. This shopping complex in the heart of Vaasa features a variety of shops, including clothing boutiques, home decor stores, and cafes.

Address: Kauppakeskus Rewell 203, Ylatori 2, 65100 Vaasa.

Seinäjoki

Seinäjoki Market Square: Dive into the vibrant atmosphere of Seinäjoki Market Square, offering a diverse range of stalls from local producers. Explore the market for fresh produce, handmade crafts, and unique finds.

Address: Kauppatori 2, 60100 Seinäjoki.

Kokkola

Charming Neristan: Stroll through the charming Neristan, Kokkola's Old Town, where boutique shops line cobblestone streets. Discover unique gifts, handmade jewelry, and antiques in this historic setting.

Oulu

Rotuaari Promenade: Wander along Rotuaari, Oulu's lively pedestrian street, dotted with shops and boutiques. Explore fashion stores, design shops, and local brands, and take in the dynamic atmosphere of the city center.

Pikisaari Island: Go to Pikisaari Island for a unique shopping experience. This historical district offers charming shops housed in old wooden buildings, selling everything from handmade crafts to vintage treasures.

Pakkahuoneenkatu Street: Explore Pakkahuoneenkatu Street, known for its boutiques and specialty stores. Find unique fashion items, home decor, and gifts while enjoying the historic surroundings.

Address: Pakkahuoneenkatu, 90100 Oulu.

Raahe

Raahe Market Square: Visit Raahe Market Square for a taste of local life. This vibrant market showcases fresh produce, local delicacies, and handmade crafts. Engage with local vendors and bring home a piece of Raahe.

Address: Pakkahuoneenkatu, 90100 Oulu.

Maritime Treasures

Marine Shops: Embrace the maritime heritage of Ostrobothnia by exploring marine-themed shops in coastal towns. Discover nautical decor, seafaring essentials, and unique souvenirs that capture the spirit of the region.

Did You Know?

Many shops in Ostrobothnia emphasize sustainable and locally sourced products. When shopping in the region, you not only get distinctive items but also support the community's commitment to environmental consciousness and local craftsmanship.

Accommodations

Ostrobothnia offers a range of accommodations, from cozy guesthouses with a touch of local charm to modern hotels providing comfort and convenience. Whether you prefer a seaside retreat or a stay in the heart of a historic town, the region has options to suit every traveler's preference.

Name	Information	Address
Original Sokos Hotel Royal Vaasa (Vaasa)	Situated in the city center, this contemporary hotel offers stylish rooms, a wellness center, and convenient access to Vaasa's attractions, including the Market Square and Rewell Center.	Hovioikeudenpuistikko 18, 65100 Vaasa
Scandic Vaasa (Vaasa)	Overlooking the Gulf of Bothnia, Scandic Vaasa provides comfortable accommodations with sea views. The hotel features modern amenities, a sauna, and a central location near the train station.	Rosteninkatu 6, 65100 Vaasa
Hotel Astor Vaasa (Vaasa)	Located in a historic building, Hotel Astor Vaasa blends classic elegance with modern comforts. The hotel is within walking distance of the Vaasa Market Square and the Old Town.	Asemakatu 4, 65100 Vaasa

Original Sokos Hotel Vaakuna Seinäjoki (Seinäjoki)	Centrally located, this hotel offers a combination of contemporary design and Finnish hospitality. Guests can enjoy amenities like a rooftop terrace and proximity to Seinäjoki's attractions.	Kauppatori 3, 60100 Seinäjoki
Hotel Alma (Seinäjoki)	A boutique hotel in the heart of Seinäjoki, Hotel Alma provides individually decorated rooms and a cozy atmosphere. The hotel is near popular sites such as the Aalto Center and Lakeuden Risti Church.	Ruukintie 4, 60100 Seinäjoki
Hotel Sorsanpesä (Seinäjoki)	Nestled by Lake Tohni, Hotel Sorsanpesä offers a tranquil retreat. The lakeside setting, modern rooms, and on-site restaurant make it an ideal choice for those seeking a peaceful stay.	Tornavantie 27, 60200 Seinäjoki
Hotel Kokkola (Kokkola)	Located in the city center, Hotel Kokkola combines modern amenities with a historic atmosphere. The hotel is close to Neristan, Kokkola's Old Town,	Rantakatu 14, 67100 Kokkola

	and offers comfortable rooms with a touch of elegance.	
Original Sokos Hotel Kaarle (Kokkola)	This hotel provides a central location in Kokkola along with comfortable rooms and a relaxing sauna. It is conveniently situated near attractions such as the Kokkola Golf and Chydenius Institute.	Kauppatori 4, 67100 Kokkola
Hotel Seurahuone (Kokkola)	Housed in a charming building, Hotel Seurahuone offers cozy accommodations and a welcoming ambiance. The hotel is within walking distance of Kokkola's museums and the beautiful Neristan area.	Torikatu 24, 67100 Kokkola
Radisson Blu Hotel Oulu (Oulu)	Overlooking the Gulf of Bothnia, this modern hotel offers stylish rooms, a rooftop terrace, and proximity to Oulu's market square. The hotel's central location allows for easy access to attractions like Nallikari Beach.	Hallituskatu 1, 90100 Oulu

Original Sokos Hotel Arina (Oulu)	Situated in the city center, Hotel Arina provides contemporary rooms, a fitness center, and a popular restaurant. Oulu Cathedral and the Rotuaari pedestrian street are nearby.	Pakkahuoneenkatu 16, 90100 Oulu
Scandic Oulu (Oulu)	With a prime location near Oulu Castle and the market square, Scandic Oulu offers comfortable accommodations and a range of amenities, including a sauna and a fitness center.	Saaristonkatu 4, 90100 Oulu
Hotelli Raahen Hovi (Raahe)	Set in a historic building, Hotelli Raahen Hovi exudes Old World charm. The hotel offers comfortable rooms, a restaurant, and a central location near Raahe's attractions, including the Old Town.	Kirkkokatu 28, 92100 Raahe

Did You Know?

Many accommodations in Ostrobothnia take pride in incorporating sustainable practices, reflecting the region's commitment to environmental responsibility. When choosing a place to stay, you may find options that align with eco-friendly initiatives and local values.

Chapter 9: Itineraries and Programs

This chapter features multiple itineraries and programs to help you make the most out of your trip. You will find a blend of wilderness retreats, urban exploration, unique adventures, and cultural experiences across Finland. You can make adjustments based on your interests and the time of the year you're planning to visit.

Enjoy Finland's wilderness retreats.[74]

6-Day Itinerary in the middle of Finland

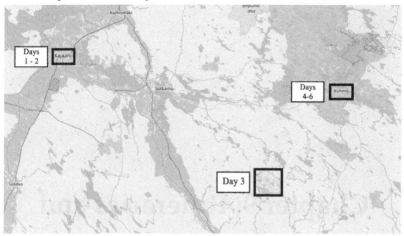

6-Day itinerary in the middle of Finland.[75]

Day 1: Arrival in Kajaani

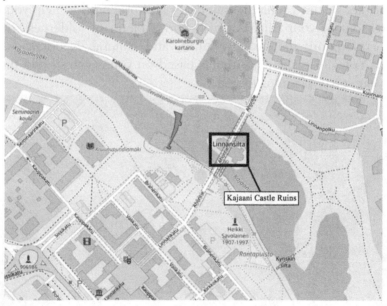

Day 1.[76]

Morning:

Arrive in the beautiful town of Kajaani and settle into your carefully chosen accommodation. For a great experience, make sure that your accommodation offers a mix of modern comfort and regional charm. Take a moment to unwind and refresh after your journey.

Afternoon:

In the afternoon, start your exploration with a visit to the historic Kajaani Castle ruins. Get involved in the tales of the past as you wander through the remnants of the medieval castle. Then, you can go for a leisurely stroll along the banks of the scenic Kajaani River and immerse yourself in the natural beauty that surrounds the town.

Kajaani Castle Ruins QR code   Kajaani River QR code.

Evening:

In the evening, you can indulge in a culinary journey through Kainuu. You can choose a traditional restaurant to enjoy the local flavors that are made from the region's rich culinary heritage.

Day 2: Take in the Culture

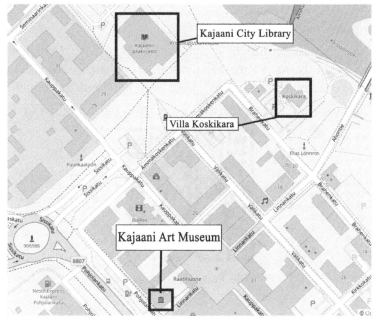

Day 2.[77]

Morning:

Start your day with a delicious breakfast at a charming local cafe to get ready for a day of cultural exploration.

Late Morning:

You must then immerse yourself in the world of art at the Kajaani Art Museum, which showcases artworks by local and international artists. You should then continue your cultural journey at the Kajaani City Library, which is a haven for literature enthusiasts, to gain an insight into the thriving local literary scene.

The Kajaani City Library is a short walk away from the Kajaani Art Museum.

Kajaani Art Museum QR Code   Kajaani City Library QR Code

Afternoon:

You can then have lunch at a local eatery before visiting the Villa Koskikara by the Kajaani River. Enjoy the serene surroundings and take a moment to contemplate and think about everything you are grateful for.

Villa Koskikara is a 5 minute walk away from the Kajaani City Library.

Villa Koskikara QR Code.

Evening:

Relax and ease into the evening at a local spa by indulging in a classic Finnish sauna experience. End your day with dinner at a traditional Finnish restaurant and relish the dishes that reflect the authentic flavors of the region.

Day 3: Hiidenportti National Park

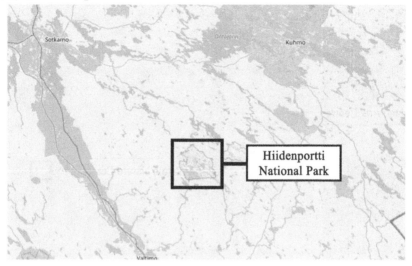

Day 3.[78]

Morning:

After having breakfast, start your nature-filled day with a journey to Hiidenportti National Park. Then, set on a morning hike, take in the beauty of waterfalls, and walk through dense forests.

Hiidenportti National Park QR Code.

Afternoon:

Take a break from your hiking adventure for a picnic lunch amid pristine surroundings. You can choose to extend your adventure or try birdwatching while taking in the calmness of the natural environment.

Evening:

As the evening falls, you can have a hearty dinner at a local grill after returning from Kajaani and share stories and reflections from your day's wilderness adventure with your loved ones.

Day 4: Kuhmo - A Cultural Hub

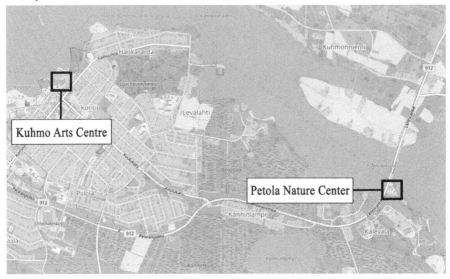

Day 4.[79]

Morning:

You can check out of your Kajaani accommodation and set out on a scenic drive to Kuhmo, which is a town rich in cultural offerings.

Late Morning:

You can then explore the Petola Nature Center and gain insight into the local wildlife and conservation efforts. Connect with the region's natural heritage through informative exhibits.

Petola Nature Center QR Code.

Afternoon:

You can have a delicious lunch in Kuhmo before going to the Kuhmo Arts Centre. There, you will be able to enjoy the impressive collection of cultural exhibits that showcase the artistic vibrancy of the region.

Kuhmo Arts Centre QR Code.

Evening:

Participate in the cultural scene with an evening event, which can be done by attending a live performance at the renowned Kuhmo Chamber Music Festival or another cultural event in the city.

The Kuhmo Chamber Music Festival is about a 450 m walk from the Kuhmo Arts Center.

Day 5: Outdoor Bliss in Kuhmo

Morning:

Start your day with a lakeside breakfast at a local cafe to prepare for a day filled with exciting outdoor activities.

Afternoon:

Go canoeing or fishing in Kuhmo's pristine lakes. You can also enjoy a little lakeside picnic for lunch and enjoy the simplicity of a meal in a natural environment.

Evening:

After a long day of physical exertion, you can indulge in a lakeside sauna to unwind from your outdoor escapades. Conclude your day with dinner at a local restaurant and appreciate the distinct flavors of Kainuu.

Day 6: Departure

Morning:

Check out of your Kuhmo accommodation and make sure you are ready to go. If time permits, visit the Kalevala Spirit exhibition, which celebrates Finnish folklore and is sure to add a magical touch to your journey.

Afternoon:

Say goodbye to Kuhmo with a farewell lunch and take in the beauty of the place during your last moments in this cultural haven.

Departure

7- Day Trip Itinerary in the south of Finland

7-day trip itinerary in the south of Finland.[80]

Day 1: Arrival in Helsinki

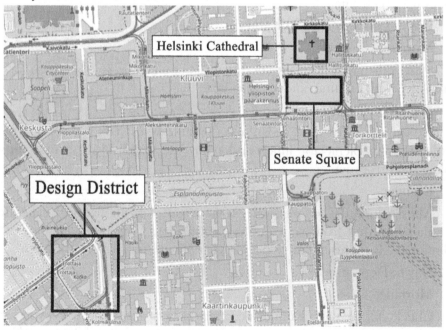

Day 1.[81]

Morning:

Begin your adventure with a warm welcome in Helsinki. Check into the hotel you carefully selected in the city center. You can then take a moment to refresh after your journey.

Afternoon:

Then, start your exploration by traveling to the historical Senate Square and Helsinki Cathedral. Take in the architectural grandeur and historical beauty of these landmarks. Then, you can enjoy a delightful lunch at a local eatery that will introduce your taste buds to Finnish flavors.

Senate Square QR Code.

Helsinki Cathedral QR Code.

Evening:

In the evening, go to the Design District to satiate your thirst for creativity. Then, start exploring the unique boutiques and design studios that showcase Finland's contemporary design scene. Then, choose a restaurant in the heart of the city for a delicious meal that is an appetizing blend of traditional and modern Finnish cuisine.

The Design District is approximately a 1.3 km walk from the Helsinki Cathedral.

Design District QR Code.

Day 2: Helsinki Highlights

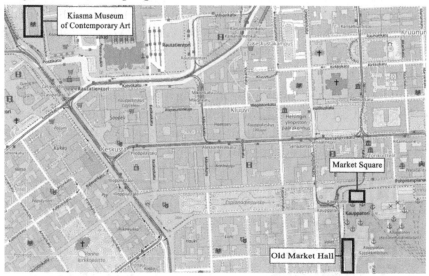

Day 2.[82]

Morning:

Start your day with a leisurely morning of shopping and coffee in this creative hub. You can choose to visit to the Kiasma Museum of Contemporary Art, which offers unique insights into Finland's artistic landscape.

Kiasma Museum of Contemporary Art QR Code.

Afternoon:

Try a leisurely lunch in the vibrant Market Square. Taste the local treats and take in the lively atmosphere of this waterfront hub. Then, take a relaxing stroll along the waterfront while admiring the views of the Baltic Sea and the city's skyline.

The Market Square is a 1.2 km walk from the Kiasma Museum of Contemporary Art.

Market Square QR Code.

Evening:

End your day with a visit to the Old Market Hall, where you can indulge in local delicacies and enjoy the diverse culinary offerings.

The Old Market Hall is a 140 m walk from the Market Square.

Old Market Hall QR Code.

Day 3: Espoo's Cultural Tapestry

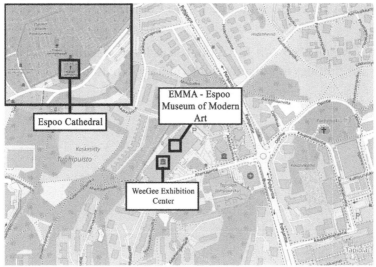

Day 3[83]

Morning

Begin your day with a visit to the EMMA – Espoo Museum of Modern Art. Allow yourself to completely immerse yourself in contemporary Finnish art and explore the thought-provoking exhibits. Then, you can continue your artistic journey with a visit to the WeeGee Exhibition Centre, which is a cultural hub showcasing a diverse range of exhibitions.

Espoo Museum of Modern Art QR Code.   WeeGee Exhibition Centre QR Code.

Afternoon:

Take a leisurely lunch in Tapiola, which is known for its cultural ambiance and charming atmosphere. Then, go on to explore the Espoo Cathedral.

To get to Tapiola from the WeeGee Exhibition Centre, walk about 900 m. To get to the Espoo Cathedral, walk about 220 m to the Hagalund (M) bus top then take bus 118 to Espoon Keskus. From there, walk approximately 650 m to get to the Espoo Cathedral.

Evening:

In the evening, go out for dinner at a local restaurant and allow the artistic surroundings to enhance your culinary experience.

Day 4: Nuuksio National Park

Day 4.[84]

Morning:

Get ready to visit the scenic Nuuksio National Park - a- a haven of natural beauty. You can check into your chosen accommodation; choose an area where you can immerse yourself deeper into the forest. Take a morning walk through the forest surroundings to connect with nature and breathe in the crisp Finnish air.

Nuuksio National Park QR Code.

Afternoon:

Enjoy a lakeside picnic while being surrounded by the serene beauty of Nuuksio. Try the local snacks and appreciate the beautiful environment. Don't forget to experience the authenticity of a traditional Finnish sauna in the afternoon and let the soothing heat relax your body and mind.

Evening:

As the evening unfolds, go on to enjoy a quiet and reflective time at your accommodation. The calm of the forest offers a perfect setting for a peaceful evening.

Day 5: Turku - Archipelago City Extravaganza

Day 5.[85]

Morning:

Set out on a scenic journey to Turku. Take a moment to fully absorb the historical charm of this beautiful town before continuing your journey. You can check into your chosen hotel in Turku, a city known for its historical significance and vibrant atmosphere.

Afternoon:

Immerse yourself in Turku's history with a visit to Turku Castle. You can explore the medieval fortress and gain insights into Finland's past. Then, you can enjoy lunch at a riverside restaurant and truly savor the fusion of historic charm and modern culinary treats.

Turku Castle QR Code.

Evening:

Get onto a sunset ferry ride in the Turku Archipelago. Allow yourself to be fully immersed and let the gentle waves and the enchanting hues of the evening sky create a magical experience.

Day 6:

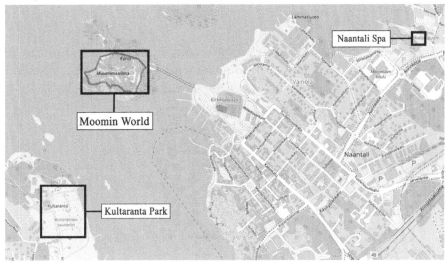

Day 6.[86]

Morning:

Set on a journey to the charming city of Naantali, a town known for its elegance and maritime allure. Then, you can choose to visit Moomin World, an amusement park inspired by Tove Jansson's beloved characters, or take a leisurely walk in the scenic Kultaranta Park.

Moomin World QR Code.

Kultaranta Park QR Code.

Afternoon:

In the afternoon, you can go on an Archipelago cruise from Naantali. There, you can explore the serene islands and relish a delectable seafood lunch on board while immersing yourself in the maritime bliss of the Archipelago Sea.

Evening:

In the evening, relax and unwind at a Naantali spa amongst the peaceful coastal surroundings. You can end your day with a seafood dinner at a local restaurant and savor the flavors of the archipelago.

Naantali Spa QR Code.

Day 7: Departure from Southwest Finland

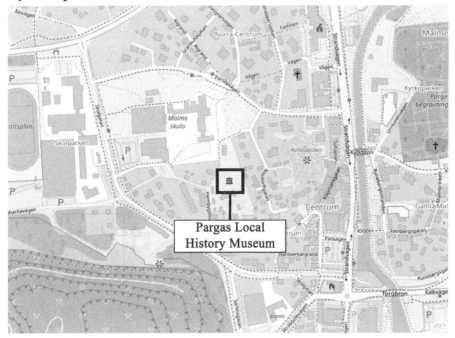

Day 7.[87]

Morning:

You can go to the Pargas and visit the Pargas Local History Museum. Immerse yourself in the rich maritime heritage of the region and gain insights into coastal traditions.

Pargas Local History Museum QR Code.

Afternoon:

Explore Pargas and soak in the coastal ambiance. Enjoy a farewell lunch in a local restaurant.

10-Day Itinerary

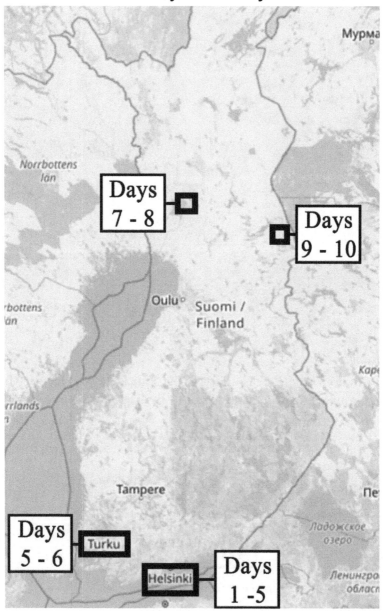

10-Day Finland itinerary.[88]

Day 1: Arrival in Helsinki

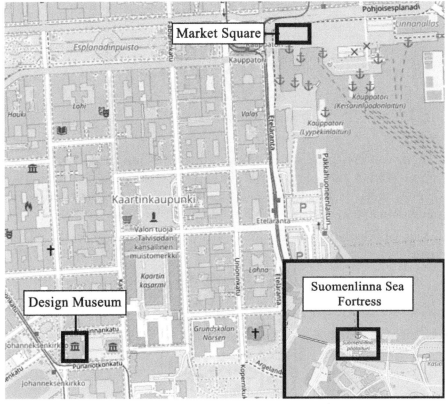

Day 1.[89]

Morning:

Arrive at Helsinki-Vantaa Airport and take in the fresh Nordic air. Then, consider getting a boutique hotel in the Design District for a touch of contemporary Finnish style. You will want to take a leisurely morning stroll around the hotel vicinity while taking in the blend of modern architecture and historical charm.

Afternoon:

You can then satiate your creative thirst by delving into the Design District. The Design Museum is a work of art as it provides an insightful journey into Finland's design legacy, from Alvar Aalto's iconic furniture to modern innovations.

Design Museum QR Code.

Evening:

Then, you can head on to Market Square, Kauppatori, for dinner at Seafood Market. Try out the fresh Finnish seafood at one of the market's charming stalls. If you feel like it, you can go on a short ferry ride to Suomenlinna Sea Fortress, a UNESCO World Heritage site.

Walk about 850 m from the Design Museum to get to the Market Square.

Suomenlinna Sea Fortress QR Code.

Day 2: Helsinki Highlights

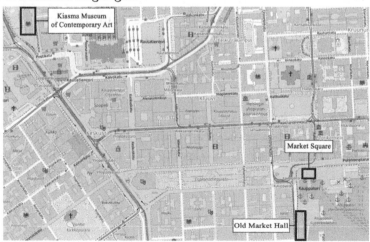

Day 2.[90]

Morning:

You can start your day with a lovely morning of shopping and coffee in this creative center. Visit the Kiasma Museum of Contemporary Art, as it will offer you a unique insight into Finland's artistic landscape.

Afternoon:

Enjoy a leisurely lunch in the vibrant Market Square. Try out the local treats and take in the lively atmosphere of this waterfront hub.

The Market Square is a 1.2 km walk from the Kiasma Museum of Contemporary Art.

Evening:

You can end your day with a visit to the Old Market Hall, which is the historic food market. Indulge in local delicacies and enjoy the diverse culinary foods.

The Old Market Hall is a 140 m walk from the Market Square.

Day 3: Nuuksio National Park

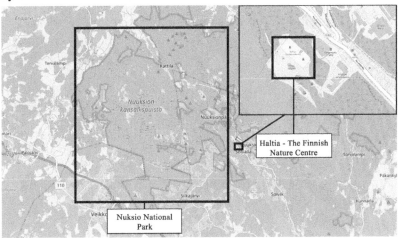

Day 3.[91]

Morning:

Say goodbye to Helsinki and set out on a scenic drive or charming train journey to Nuuksio National Park. You could get a cozy cabin among the serene Finnish nature.

Afternoon:

Start your hiking journey in Nuuksio through lush green forests and beautiful lakes. You can visit the Haltia - The Finnish Nature Centre for a deeper understanding of the local flora and fauna.

Walk approximately 240 m from Nuuksio to get to Haltia – The Finnish Nature Centre.

Haltia – The Finnish Nature Centre QR Code.

Evening:

Surrender to the Finnish tradition of sauna. You can unwind in the warmth of a traditional sauna while being surrounded by nature.

Day 4: Wilderness Adventures Continue

Morning:

Start your morning with a delicious breakfast at your wilderness cabin. Then, engage in morning activities, like birdwatching or exploring nearby trails.

Afternoon:

You can choose to have a picnic lunch in the heart of nature while being surrounded by the beauty of Nuuksio. Then, continue your hike or try birdwatching in the serene surroundings.

Evening:

Then, you can return to Helsinki for a hearty dinner at a local grill.

Day 5: Turku

Morning:

Set out on a journey to Turku, which is Finland's oldest city known for its cobblestone streets and medieval architecture.

Afternoon:

Get on a cruise ship for an enchanting voyage through the Turku Archipelago. Select an island, such as Naantali, to explore.

Evening:

You can then take a walk along the Aura River as the sun sets, where historic buildings and modern art coexist harmoniously. Then, you can choose a riverside restaurant for a delightful dinner.

Day 6: History of Turku

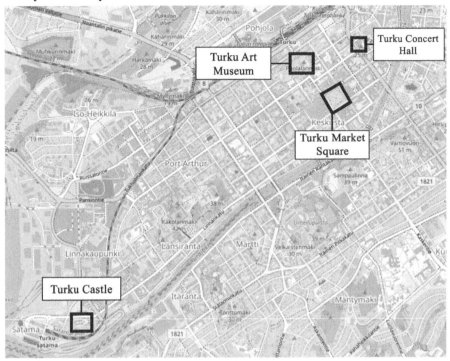

Day 6.[92]

Morning:

Explore Turku Castle, a medieval fortress with a rich history. You can then stroll along the Aura River and explore the Turku Market Square.

Walk 160 m from the Turku Castle to the Hamngatan bus stop and take bus 1 (Airport) to the Market Square (City Centre) A2 stop then walk about 160 m to get to the Turku Market Square.

Turku Market Square QR Code.

Afternoon:

Enjoy lunch at a waterside restaurant and later dive into Turku's cultural scene with a visit to the Turku Art Museum.

Walk 350 m from the Turku Market Square to the Turku Art Museum.

Turku Art Museum QR Code.

Evening:

You can later attend a live performance at the renowned Turku Concert Hall or another cultural event in the city.

Walk 600 m from the Turku Art Museum to the Turku Concert Hall.

Turku Concert Hall QR Code.

Day 7: Flight to Rovaniemi

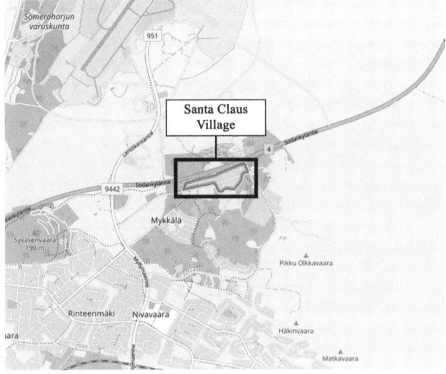

Day 7.[93]

Morning:

Take a flight to Rovaniemi, the official hometown of Santa Claus and the gateway to Lapland.

Afternoon:

Get on a whimsical visit to Santa Claus Village, where the Christmas spirit is alive year-round.

Santa Claus Village QR Code.

Evening:

Start your journey with the guided Northern Lights safari. Follow the aurora borealis as it dances across the Arctic sky.

Day 8: Lapland Wonders Continue

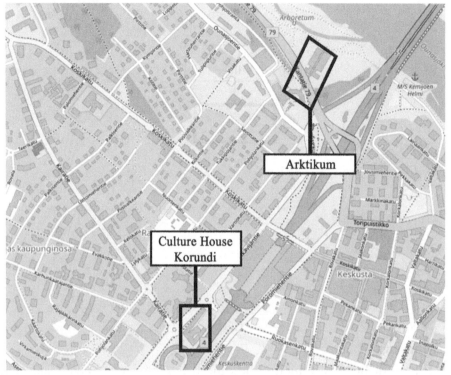

Day 8.[94]

Morning:

You can enjoy a leisurely morning in Rovaniemi to explore local cafes and shops. You can visit the Arktikum Science Museum for insights into Lapland's unique nature and culture.

Arktikum Science Museum QR Code.

Afternoon:

Have lunch at a traditional Lappish restaurant and savor the local delicacies. Then, explore the Culture House Korundi.

Walk 900 m from the Arktikum Science Museum to reach Culture House Korundi.

Culture House Korundi QR Code.

Ranua Wildlife Park QR Code.

Evening:

Return to your accommodations for a cozy evening and sit by the fireplace with a coffee.

Day 9: Kuusamo Bound

Morning:

You should then get ready to fly to Kuusamo, which is a haven for nature enthusiasts.

Afternoon:

Set on a bear-watching excursion in the nearby forests. You can silently observe these majestic creatures in their natural habitat with the help of experts.

Evening:

Pick anywhere you like for the last dinner of your vacation.

Day 10: Farewell to Finland

Morning:

Take a moment to take in the beauty of Kuusamo's wilderness while enjoying a leisurely farewell breakfast at your wilderness lodge.

Afternoon:

Go to Kuusamo Airport for your departure and reflect on the incredible experiences and memories created during your 10-day adventure in Finland.

Bonus Chapter: Useful Finnish Survival Phrases

Learning basic Finnish will be extremely important for you as a traveler as it helps you communicate easily with the locals. While English is widely spoken in Finland, people will undoubtedly appreciate your knowledge of these phrases. It will help you connect better with the locals. Acquiring fundamental knowledge of basic Finnish phrases will enhance your interaction and help you foster a deeper understanding of the culture while allowing you to have a more meaningful bond with locals.

Learn basic Finnish phrases.[95]

Phrases to Remember

Greetings

- **Hello** - hei / moi (hey / moy).
- **Good Morning** - Hyvää huomenta (huu-vaa hoo-oh-mehn-tah).
- **Good Night** - yvää yötä (huu-vaa uu-euh-ta).
- **Good Evening** - Hyvää iltaa (huu-vaa eel-tah).
- **Goodbye** - Hei / moi (hey / moy moy).
- **How Are You?** - Mitä kuuluu? (mee-ta kooh-looh).
- **I Am Very Well, Thank You** - Oikein hyvää, kiitos (oy-keh-in huu-vaa, kee-tohss).
- **Good, Thank You** - Hyvää, kiitos (huu-vaa, kee-tohss).
- **What Is Your Name?** - Mikä sinun nimesi on? (mee-ka see-noon nee-meh-see ohn).
- **My Name Is...** - Minun nimeni on... (mee-noon nee-meh-nee ohn).
- **It's Nice to Meet You** - Hauska tutustua (how-skah too-toos-too-ah).

Farewells

- **Goodbye** - Näkemiin (Nah-keh-meen).
- **Farewell** - Hyvästi (Huu-vahs-tee).
- **See You Later** - Nähdään myöhemmin (Nahd-aan myo-hehm-meen).
- **Until We Meet Again** - Siihen asti kunnes tavataan uudelleen (See-hehn ah-stee koon-nehs tah-vah-taan oo-deh-leh-en).
- **Take Care** - Ole varovainen (Oh-leh vah-roh-vahy-nehn).
- **Have a Good Journey** - Hyvää matkaa (Huu-vaa maht-kah).
- **Good Luck** - Onnea (Ohn-neh-ah).
- **Safe Travels** - Turvallista matkaa (Tur-vahl-lee-stah maht-kah).
- **See You Soon** - Nähdään pian (Nahd-aan pee-ahn).
- **Until Next Time** - Seuraavaan kertaan asti (Seh-oo-rah-vaa-ahn kehr-tahn ah-stee).

Essentials:

- **Thank You** - Kiitos (kee-tohss).
- **You're Welcome** - Ole hyvä / eipä kestä (oh-lay huu-va / ay-pa kehss-ta).
- **Ok** - Ok / okei (oh-koh / oh-kay).
- **Excuse Me** - Anteeksi (ahn-teh-xee).
- **I'm Sorry** - Anteeksi (ahn-teh-xee).
- **I Don't Understand** - En ymmärrä (ehn-ummar-ra).
- **I Only Speak a Little Bit of Finnish** - Puhun vain vähän suomea (poo-hoon vah-een va-han soo-oh-meh-ah).
- **Can You Please Repeat That Slowly** - Voisitko toistaa hitaasti? (voh-ee-seet-koh toh-ee-staah hee-taahs-tee?).

Questions:

- **Where?** - Missä? (mees-sa?).
- **How?** - Miten? (mee-tehn?).
- **Where Is/Are...?** - Missä on...? (mees-sa ohn...?).
- **How Much?** - Kuinka paljon? (koo-een-kah pahl-yohn?).
- **Who?** - Kuka? (koo-kah?).
- **When?** - Milloin? (meel-loh-een?).
- **Why?** - Miksi? (meek-see?).
- **What?** - Mitä? (mee-ta?).
- **Which?** - Mikä? (mee-ka?).
- **How Much Is This?** - Paljonko tämä maksaa? (pahl-yohn-koh ta-ma mahk-sah?).
- **How Much Does That Cost?** - Paljonko tuo maksaa? (pahl-yohn-koh too-oh mahk-sah?).
- **Where Is the Toilet?** - Missä on vessa? (mees-sa ohn vehs-sah?).
- **Can I Have...** - Saisinko... (sigh-seen-koh...).
- **I Would Like...** - Haluaisin... (hah-loo-i-seen...).

Food and Drink:

- **The Menu, Please** - Saisinko ruokalistan (sigh-seen-koh roo-oh-kah-lees-tahn).

- **Two Beers, Please** - Kaksi olutta, kiitos (kahk-see oh-loot-tah, kee-tohss).

- **A Bottle of House White/Red Wine, Please** - Pullo talon valkoviiniä/punaviiniä, kiitos (pool-loh tah-lohn vahl-koh-vee-nee-ya, kee-tohss).

- **Some Water, Please** - Vettä, kiitos (veht-ta, kee-tohss).

- **I'm Allergic to...** - Olen allerginen... (oh-lehn ahl-lehr-ghee-nehn).

- **I'm a Vegetarian** - Olen kasvissyöjä (oh-lehn kahs-vees-suu-euh-ya).

- **Can We Have the Bill, Please?** - Saisimmeko laskun? (sigh-seem-meh-koh lahs-koon?).

- **What Do You Recommend?** - Mitä te suosittelette? (mee-ta teh soo-oh-seet-teh-leht-teh?).

- **The Meal Was Excellent** - Ruoka oli erinomaista (roo-oh-kah oh-lee eh-ree-noh-mah-ees-tah).

Getting Around:

- **Left** - Vasen (vah-sehn).

- **Right** - Oikea (oy-keh-ah).

- **Straight Ahead** - Suoraan eteenpäin (soo-oh-rahn eh-tehn-pain).

- **Turn Left** - Käänny vasemmalle (kaan-nu vah-sehm-mahl-leh).

- **Turn Right** - Käänny oikealle (kaan-nu oy-keh-ahl-leh).

- **Bus Stop** - Bussipysäkki (boos-see-pu-sak-kee).

- **Train Station** - Juna-asema (yuh-nah-ah-seh-mah).

- **Airport** - Lentokenttä (lehn-toh-kehnt-ta).

- **Entrance** - Sisäänkäynti (see-san-ka-uun-tee).

- **Exit** - Uloskäynti (uh-lohs-ka-uun-tee).

Emergency:

- **Help!** - Apua! (ah-poo-ah!).

- **I Need a Doctor** - Tarvitsen lääkäriä (tahr-veet-sehn laa-kaa-ree-ya).

- **I Don't Feel Well** - Voin huonosti (voh-een hoo-oh-noh-stee).

- **Call the Police!** - Kutsukaa poliisi! (koot-soo-kaah poh-lee-see).

- **There's a Fire!** - Tulipalo! (too-lee-pah-loh!).

Seeking Help:

- **Can You Help Me, Please?** - Voisitko auttaa minua, kiitos? (Voi-sit-koh aut-taa mee-nua, kee-tohs?).

- **I Need Help.** - Tarvitsen apua. (Tar-vit-sen ah-pua.).

- **Is There Someone Who Speaks English?** - Onko täällä jotain, joka puhuu englantia? (On-koh tael-lae yot-ain, yo-ka poo-hoo eng-lan-ti-ah?).

- **I'm Lost.** - Olen eksyksissä. (O-lenn eks-uk-sis-sa.).

- **Can You Show Me on the Map?** - Voitko näyttää sen kartalta? (Voi-tko nayt-taa sen kar-tal-ta?).

- **I'm Not Feeling Well.** - En voi kovin hyvin. (En voi koh-vin huu-vin.).

- **Could You Please Call a Doctor?** - Voisitteko soittaa lääkärille? (Voi-sit-te-ko soit-taa leh-kah-ri-le?).

- **I Need to Contact the Embassy.** - Minun täytyy ottaa yhteyttä suurlähetystöön. (Mee-nun tait-toi ot-taa yh-tey-ta soo-ur-la-het-is-tohn.).

Small Talk:

- **Where Are You from?** - Mistä olet kotoisin? (Mees-tah oh-let koh-toh-ee-seen?).

- **I'm from [Country].** - Olen kotoisin [maasta]. (Oh-lehn koh-toh-ee-seen [maa-sta]).

- **What Do You Do for a Living?** - Mitä teet työksesi? (Mee-ta teht tyyrk-seh-ksi?).

- **I Work as a [Profession].** - Työskentelen [ammatti]. (Tyyr-skent-e-lehn [am-mat-tee]).

- **How's the Weather Today?** - Minkälainen sää tänään on? (Mink-ah-lai-nen seh tah-nayn on?).

- **What Do You Like to Do for Fun?** - Mitä tykkäät tehdä vapaa-ajallasi? (Mee-ta tyy-kaat teh-dah vah-paa-ah-yal-la-see?).

- **Do You Have Any Hobbies?** - Onko sinulla harrastuksia? (On-koh see-noo-lah har-ras-took-see-ah?).

- **Have You Been to [Place]?** - Oletko käynyt [paikassa]? (Oh-let-koh kai-nyt [paik-as-sa]?).

- **What's Your Favorite [Food, Movie, Book, Etc.]?** - Mikä on suosikkisi [ruoka, elokuva, kirja, jne.]? (Mik-ah on soo-osik-ki-see [roo-oh-ka, eh-loh-koo-vah, keer-yah, yh-nee]?).

- **That Sounds Interesting!** - Kuulostaa mielenkiintoiselta! (Koo-loh-stah mee-len-kin-toy-sehl-tah!).

- **How Was Your Weekend?** - Miten viikonloppusi meni? (Mee-ten vee-kon-lop-poo-see men-ee?).

- **Do You Have Any Upcoming Plans?** - Onko sinulla tulevia suunnitelmia? (On-koh see-noo-lah too-lev-ee-ah soon-nee-tehl-mee-ah?).

- **I Love the Scenery Here.** - Rakastan tätä maisemaa. (Rah-kas-tan ta-ta mahy-seh-maa).

- **What Languages Do You Speak?** - Mitä kieliä puhut? (Mee-ta kee-eh-lee-ah poo-hoot?).

Common Words to Know

Numbers:

- **One** - Yksi (Uuk-si).
- **Two** - Kaksi (Kak-si).
- **Three** - Kolme (Kol-meh).
- **Four** - Neljä (Nel-yah).
- **Five** - Viisi (Vii-si).
- **Six** - Kuusi (Kuu-si).
- **Seven** - Seitsemän (Sait-seh-mahn).
- **Eight** - Kahdeksan (Kah-dek-san).

- **Nine** - Yhdeksän (Uuh-dek-sahn).
- **Ten** - Kymmenen (Kum-meh-nen).

Days of the Week

- **Monday** - Maanantai (Mah-ah-nahn-tai).
- **Tuesday** - Tiistai (Tee-is-tai).
- **Wednesday** - Keskiviikko (Kesk-ee-veek-koh).
- **Thursday** - Torstai (Tor-stai).
- **Friday** - Perjantai (Per-yahn-tai).
- **Saturday** - Lauantai (Lau-an-tai).
- **Sunday** - Sunnuntai (Soon-oon-tai).

Time

- **What Time Is It?** - Mitä kello on? (Mee-ta kel-lo on?).
- **It's One O'clock.** - On yksi. (On uuk-si.).
- **It's Half Past Two.** - On puoli kolme. (On pwoh-lee kol-meh.).
- **It's Quarter Past Three.** - On varttia yli kolme. (On vart-tee-ah y-lee kol-meh.).
- **It's Ten Minutes to Four.** - On kymmenen minuuttia vaille neljä. (On kum-meh-nen mee-noot-tee-ah vai-lleh nel-ya.).
- **In the Morning** - Aamulla (Ah-ah-mul-la).
- **In the Afternoon** - Iltapäivällä (Eel-tah-pa-i-vel-lah).
- **In the Evening** - Illalla (Eel-lah-lah).
- **At Night** - Yöllä (Y-uh-lah).
- **What Time Do You Usually [Do Something]?** - Mihin aikaan yleensä [teet jotain]? (Mih-hin ai-ka-an y-leen-sah [teet yot-ai-n]?).

Shopping:

- **How Much Does This Cost?** - Paljonko tämä maksaa? (Pall-yon-koh tah-ma mahk-sah-ah?).
- **I Would Like to Buy [Item].** - Haluaisin ostaa [tuote]. (Hah-lu-ai-sin os-taa [tu-o-te].).
- **Can I Pay with a Credit Card?** - Voinko maksaa luottokortilla? (Voin-koh mahk-saa loo-toh-kor-til-la?).

- **Do You Accept Cash?** - Hyväksyttekö käteistä? (Huu-vak-sut-teh-koh kah-tai-sta?).
- **Where Is the Nearest Supermarket/Market?** - Missä on lähin supermarket/marketti? (Mees-sah on lay-hin soo-per-mar-ket/mar-ket-tee?).
- **Is There a Discount on This Item?** - Onko tällä tuotteella alennusta? (On-koh tahl-lah too-o-teh-el-lah ah-len-noo-sta?).
- **Could I Try This on?** - Voinko kokeilla tätä päällä? (Voin-koh koh-kay-il-la ta-ta pie-al-la?).
- **Do You Have This in a Different Color/Size?** - Onko tätä eri väriä/kokoa? (On-koh ta-ta eh-ri vair-ee-ah/ko-koh-ah?).
- **I'm Just Browsing.** - Selailen vain. (Sail-eye-len vain.).
- **Thank You, I'll Take It.** - Kiitos, otan sen. (Kee-tohs, oh-tan sen.).

Transportation:

- **Where Is the Bus/Train Station?** - Missä on bussi/juna-asema? (Mees-sah on boos-see/yoo-na ah-seh-mah?).
- **How Much Is a Ticket to [Destination]?** - Paljonko maksaa lippu [kohteeseen]? (Pall-yon-koh mahk-saa lip-poo [koh-teh-seen]?).
- **When Is the Next Bus/Train to [Destination]?** - Milloin on seuraava bussi/juna [kohteeseen]? (Mee-lloin on seh-oo-rah-ah-vah boos-see/yoo-na [koh-teh-seen]?).
- **Is There a Taxi Stand Nearby?** - Onko tässä lähellä taksiasema? (On-koh tahs-sah layh-lah tahk-si-ah-seh-mah?).
- **How Much Does It Cost to Go to [Destination] By Taxi?** - Paljonko maksaa matka [kohteeseen] taksilla? (Pall-yon-koh mahk-saa maht-kah [koh-teh-seen] tahk-sil-lah?).
- **I Would Like to Go to the Airport.** - Haluaisin mennä lentokentälle. (Hah-lu-ai-sin men-na len-toh-ken-tal-le.).
- **Where Can I Rent a Car?** - Mistä voin vuokrata auton? (Mees-tah voin voo-krah-tah ow-tohn?).
- **Is There a Subway/Metro Station Here?** - Onko täällä metroasema? (On-koh tah-el-lah meh-tro-ah-seh-mah?).

- **Which Platform Does the Train/Bus Leave From?** - Mistä laituri/osa lähtee juna/bussi? (Mees-tah lie-too-ree/oh-sah joo-nah/boos-see?).

- Excuse me, is this the right way to [location]? - Anteeksi, onko tämä oikea tie [paikkaan]? (An-tehk-see, on-koh tah-mah oy-keh-ah tee [pah-ik-kahn]?)

Accommodation:

- **Do You Have Any Available Rooms?** - Onko teillä vapaita huoneita? (On-koh tayl-lah vah-pai-ta hoo-o-neh-ei-ta?).

- **How Much Is a Night?** - Paljonko maksaa yö? (Pall-yon-koh mahk-saa y-uh?).

- **Is Breakfast Included?** - Sisältyykö aamiainen? (Sis-ahl-tuuk-ko ah-mee-nen?).

- **What Time Is Check-in/Check-Out?** - Milloin sisäänkirjautuminen/uloskirjautuminen on? (Mee-lloin sis-aan-keer-jau-too-mi-nen/oo-los-keer-jau-too-mi-nen on?).

- **I Have a Reservation.** - Minulla on varaus. (Mee-nul-lah on va-raus.).

- **Can I See the Room First?** - Voinko nähdä huoneen ensin? (Voin-koh naa-dah hoo-o-nehn ens-in?).

- **Is There Free Wi-Fi?** - Onko ilmainen Wi-Fi? (On-koh eel-mai-nen Wi-Fi?).

- **Is There a Parking Space Available?** - Onko saatavilla pysäköintitilaa? (On-koh saa-tah-vil-la puu-saa-kein-tee-ah-lah?).

- **Can You Recommend a Good Restaurant Nearby?** - Voitteko suositella hyvää ravintolaa lähellä? (Voi-teh-koh soo-soi-tel-lah huu-vaa ra-vin-to-laa layh-lah?).

- **The Room Is Too Hot/Cold.** - Huone on liian kuuma/kylmä. (Hoo-o-ne on lee-i-an koo-ma/kool-ma.).

Appendix

Conclusion

Having traversed the pages of this comprehensive travel guide, you've been immersed in the diverse regions that define the heart and soul of Finland. From the dynamic energy of bustling urban centers to the serene tranquility of hidden rural retreats, you've explored a kaleidoscope of attractions, each adding its own unique charm.

A Glimpse into Finland's Past

Travel back into Finland's rich history, from ancient tales to modern narratives, discovering the threads that weave its cultural landscape. Whether exploring historical landmarks or immersing yourself in cultural heritage sites, this book is your guide to Finland's captivating history.

Navigating the Skies

From major international hubs connecting you to the heart of the country to regional airports facilitating seamless transitions between regions, the guide's detailed information guarantees that your journey starts and concludes with both efficiency and ease.

Must-See Attractions

From the iconic historical landmarks to the lesser-known hidden gems, you learned about the full spectrum of experiences Finland has to offer, whether standing in awe of the historical charm of Turku or marveling at the natural splendor of Lapland.

Transportation

Navigating the intricate transportation networks, from modern urban metros to scenic train routes, allows you to focus on the adventure at hand.

Shopping and Entertainment

Think back on the hidden shopping gems and vibrant entertainment scenes you encountered. Whether exploring local markets for traditional crafts or immersing yourself in the cultural events of modern districts, your journey was enriched by a diverse tapestry of immersive experiences and retreats and feasts.

Accommodation Section

Whether you find comfort in boutique hotels within bustling city centers or tranquility in charming bed and breakfasts nestled in scenic landscapes, you are bound to find something you like.

Where to Eat

From savoring local delicacies at street food stalls to indulging in regional specialties at fine dining establishments, each dining experience becomes a flavorful chapter in your exploration of the country's diverse gastronomic landscape.

Language Toolkit

As you conclude this travelogue, remember the dedicated chapter on essential phrases, words, and sentences. The linguistic toolkit served as a bridge, allowing you to navigate unfamiliar streets, connect with locals, and handle unexpected situations with confidence, ensuring you communicated and navigated with finesse.

As you close the chapters of this guide, you've not only read about the regions but have lived through the experiences, with the aim to make your vacation an intricate and memorable journey through the captivating landscapes and culture of this remarkable country.

If you enjoyed this book, a review on Amazon would be greatly appreciated because it would mean a lot to hear from you.

To leave a review:

1. Open your camera app.
2. Point your mobile device at the QR code.
3. The review page will appear in your web browser.

Thanks for your support!

Here's another book by Captivating Travels that you might like

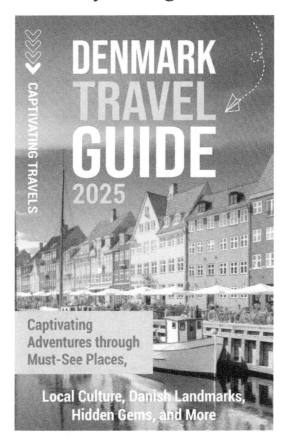

Welcome Aboard, Discover Your Limited-Time Free Bonus!

Hello, traveler! Welcome to the Captivating Travels family, and thanks for grabbing a copy of this book! Since you've chosen to join us on this journey, we'd like to offer you something special.

Check out the link below for a **FREE** Ultimate Travel Checklist eBook & Printable PDF to make your travel planning stress-free and enjoyable.

But that's not all - you'll also gain access to our exclusive email list with even more free e-books and insider travel tips. Well, what are you waiting for? Click the link below to join and embark on your next adventure with ease.

Access your bonus here:
https://livetolearn.lpages.co/checklist/
Or, Scan the QR code!

References

10 Best Ski Resorts in Finland | Visit Finland. (n.d.). https://www.visitfinland.com/en/articles/best-ski-resorts-in-finland/

12 Things to Do on a Layover at Helsinki Airport. (n.d.). Sleeping in Airports. https://www.sleepinginairports.net/layovers/things-to-do-on-a-layover-helsinki-airport.htm

14 Top Tourist Attractions in Finland. (2018, May 18). Touropia. https://www.touropia.com/tourist-attractions-in-finland/

Ahlberg, M. (2020, October 19). What Do People in Finland Do in Their Free Time? - thisisFINLAND. thisisFINLAND. https://finland.fi/facts-stats-and-info/what-do-people-in-finland-do-in-their-free-time/

Alano, M. (2023, December 4). Public Transportation in Finland: Everything You Need to Know for a Smooth Journey Around the Country This 2024! Edunation. https://www.edunation.co/blog/public-transportation-in-finland/#:~:text=Trains%20are%20the%20go%2Dto,drinks%20for%20long%2Ddistance%20travel.

Attractions and Places To See Around Kainuu - Top 20 | Komoot. (n.d.). Komoot. https://www.komoot.com/guide/902029/attractions-around-kainuu

Backman, T. (2023, May 5). Finland – A True Hockey Nation - Coastline. Coastline. https://www.coastline.fi/a-hockey-nation/

City Labs. (n.d.). Smart City Espoo. Smart City Espoo | Nordic Smart City Network. https://nscn.eu/espoo

Country and Territory Profiles - SNG-WOFI - FINLAND - EUROPE. (n.d.). https://www.sng-wofi.org/country-profiles/finland.html

Day Trips: Loviisa. My Helsinki. (n.d.). https://www.myhelsinki.fi/en/see-and-do/daytrips/day-trips-loviisa

Devesh. (2023, November 20). The Perfect 10-Day Finland Winter Itinerary. Drone & DSLR. https://droneandslr.com/travel-blog/finland/10-day-winter-itinerary/

Eight Coolest Eateries in Lapland | Visit Finnish Lapland. (2017, September 5). House of Lapland. https://www.lapland.fi/visit/tips-stories/8-coolest-eateries-in-lapland/

Emma - Espoo Museum of Modern Art Espoo. Discovering Finland. (n.d.-a). https://www.discoveringfinland.com/destination/emma-espoo-museum-of-modern-art/

Espoo Finland Tourism - Best Things To Do In Espoo. Discovering Finland. (n.d.-b). https://www.discoveringfinland.com/metropolitan-area/espoo/

Fall In Love With Helsinki. My Helsinki. (n.d.-a). https://www.myhelsinki.fi/en/your-local-guide-to-helsinki

Finnish Aviation Museum. IZI Travel. (n.d.). https://izi.travel/en/d3a5-finnish-aviation-museum/en

Finnish Roadtrip. (2019, July 18). Live Eat Colour. https://liveeatcolour.com/tag/finnish-roadtrip/

Food and Culture Along the Via Karelia Route. (2021, May 26). Discovering Finland. https://www.discoveringfinland.com/blog/food-culture-karelia-route/

General Info on Kauniainen. Kauniainen. (n.d.). https://www.kauniainen.fi/en/the-city-and-public-decision-making/general-info-on-kauniainen/

Get Talking: The Top Finnish Phrases For Beginners. FinnishPod101.com Blog. (2022, February 1). https://www.finnishpod101.com/blog/2022/01/28/finnish-beginner-phrases/

Getting Around Helsinki. (n.d.). My Helsinki. https://www.myhelsinki.fi/en/info/getting-around-helsinki#Saariliikenne

Hakala, A. (2023, March 8). Food in Finland: 5 Factors that Define Finnish Cuisine. Silk Road Workforce Management. https://workinfinland.silkroad.fi/food-in-finland/

Helsinki Airport - Everything You Need To Know | Helsinki-Vantaa Airport. (n.d.). Www.finnstyle.com. https://www.finnstyle.com/helsinki-vantaa-airport.html

Helsinki Skyline: The 50 Most Iconic Buildings And Best Views In Helsinki. (n.d.). Wanderlog. https://wanderlog.com/list/geoCategory/111883/helsinki-skyline-most-iconic-buildings-and-best-views-in-helsinki

Helsinki Travel Guide: What To Do In Helsinki. Rough Guides. (n.d.). https://www.roughguides.com/finland/helsinki/#what-to-see-and-do

Helsinki's Best Venues For Live Gigs. (n.d.). My Helsinki. https://www.myhelsinki.fi/en/eat-and-drink/bars-and-nightlife/helsinki%E2%80%99s-best-venues-for-live-gigs

History of Helsinki in a Nutshell. My Helsinki. (n.d.-c). https://www.myhelsinki.fi/en/info/history-of-helsinki-in-a-nutshell

Hostels Worldwide - Online Hostel Bookings, Ratings And Reviews. Hostelworld.com. (n.d.). https://www.hostelworld.com/st/hostels/p/1912/eurohostel-helsinki/

Hunter, M. (2023, March 20). The World's Happiest Countries for 2023. CNN. https://edition.cnn.com/travel/article/world-happiest-countries-2023-wellness/index.html

Iamjolow. (2019, December 9). Things You Need to Know Before Visiting Finland, Lapland. OUR TRAVEL ITINERARY. http://www.ourtravelitinerary.com/2016/01/things-you-need-to-know-before-visiting.html

Interesting Facts about Finnish Culture You Probably Haven't Heard Before. (2021, December 3). Helsinki Times. https://www.helsinkitimes.fi/culture/20511-interesting-facts-about-finnish-culture-you-probably-haven-t-heard-before.html

Kathrin. (2023, October 23). The Best Finnish Restaurants in Helsinki. Kathrin deter -. https://kathrindeter.com/the-best-finnish-restaurants-in-helsinki/

Kauniainen Travel Guide: Best Of Kauniainen, Uusimaa Travel 2024. Expedia.co.uk. (n.d.). https://www.expedia.co.uk/Kauniainen.dx178662

King, S. (2023, June 4). Day Trips from Helsinki. Travelling King. https://www.travellingking.com/day-trips-from-helsinki/

Kirkkonummi Area. Visit Espoo. (n.d.). https://www.visitespoo.fi/en/visitor/see-do/sights-attractions/kirkkonummi-area

Lapland. (n.d.). Www.visitfinland.com. https://www.visitfinland.com/en/places-to-go/lapland/

Leasca, S. (2023, November 2). How to Plan the Perfect Trip to Finnish Lapland — Northern Lights and Midnight Sun Included. Travel + Leisure. https://www.travelandleisure.com/lapland-finland-travel-guide-6890573

Mapes, T. (2019, August 9). Useful Finnish Words and Phrases for Traveling. TripSavvy. https://www.tripsavvy.com/useful-words-and-phrases-in-finnish-suomi-1626420

Maternity Package 2022. (n.d.). Kela. https://www.kela.fi/maternity-package-2022

Nature: How Connecting with Nature Benefits Our Mental Health. (n.d.). Mental Health Foundation. https://www.mentalhealth.org.uk/our-work/research/nature-how-connecting-nature-benefits-our-mental-health

Naturetravels. (2023, May 16). Basic Finnish Phrases for Visiting Finland. Nature Travels Blog. https://www.naturetravels.co.uk/blog/basic-finnish-phrases/

Nolan, B. (2023, December 25). Finnish People May Be Some of the Happiest in the World But They Also Have Several Unusual Traditions. Here Are 5 Surprising Facts about the World's Happiest Country. Business Insider. https://www.businessinsider.com/5-surprising-facts-about-finland-the-worlds-happiest-country-2023-6

Norah, L. (2023, December 15). The Ultimate 7 Day Finnish Lapland Itinerary for Winter + Map And Tips. Finding the Universe. https://www.findingtheuniverse.com/finland-itinerary-winter/

Paananen, A. (2023, May 25). 10 Things to Know Before Visiting Finland – Tips From a Local. Spend Life Traveling. https://www.spendlifetraveling.com/things-to-know-before-traveling-to-finland/

Parker, S. (2023, April 7). Ultimate 1 Week Finland Itinerary. Big World Small Pockets. https://www.bigworldsmallpockets.com/finland-itinerary/

Pegasus. (n.d.). Helsinki Travel Guide. Www.flypgs.com. https://www.flypgs.com/en/city-guide/helsinki-travel-guide

Sipoo. Eurocities. (2021, January 21). https://eurocities.eu/cities/sipoo/

Talen, R. (2023, January 13). 10 Days In Finland - 5 Unique Itinerary Ideas. kimkim. https://www.kimkim.com/c/10-days-in-finland-unique-itineraries

Telegraph Media Group. (2016, April 15). Best Hotels in Helsinki. The Telegraph. https://www.telegraph.co.uk/travel/destinations/europe/finland/helsinki/hotels/

Teslaru, A. (2020, March 21). 21 EPIC Things to do in Lapland (Finland) in Winter 2023. Daily Travel Pill. https://dailytravelpill.com/things-to-do-in-lapland/

THE 10 BEST Hotels in Suomussalmi, Finland 2024 (from $91). (n.d.). Tripadvisor. https://www.tripadvisor.com/Hotels-g1598850-Suomussalmi_Wild_Taiga_Kainuu-Hotels.html

THE 10 BEST Restaurants in Central Finland (Updated January 2024). (n.d.). Tripadvisor. https://www.tripadvisor.com/Restaurants-g8659045-Central_Finland.html

THE 15 BEST Things to Do in Ostrobothnia - 2024 (with Photos). (n.d.). Tripadvisor. https://www.tripadvisor.com/Attractions-g8659037-Activities-Ostrobothnia.html

The National Museum of Finland. (n.d.). Hvitträsk. https://www.kansallismuseo.fi/en/hvittraesk

The Official Naantali Tourist Information. Visit Naantali. (2023, November 13). https://visitnaantali.com/en/

Theintrepidguide. (2021, May 23). 99 Phrases In Finnish You Should Know

Before Visiting Finland [bonus audio]. The Intrepid Guide. https://www.theintrepidguide.com/phrases-in-finnish/

Top Shopping Centres in Helsinki. (n.d.). Www.inyourpocket.com. https://www.inyourpocket.com/helsinki/top-shopping-centres-in-helsinki_77048f

Tourism Uusikaupunki - Uusikaupunki Travel Guide. Discovering Finland. (n.d.-c). https://www.discoveringfinland.com/southern-finland-archipelago/uusikaupunki/

Turner, A. (2021, April 26). North Finland | Finland Travel Guide. Rough Guides. https://www.roughguides.com/finland/north/

Varpu. (2018, December 11). The Ultimate Guide to Helsinki Airport. Her Finland. https://herfinland.com/helsinki-airport-ultimate-guide/

Ville Palonen. (2021, April 20). Wild East – Kainuu and North Karelia Regions of Eastern Finland. Featuring Finland. https://featuringfinland.com/east-finland-kainuu-karelia-travel-guide/

VISIT SALO. (2019). https://visitsalo.fi/wp-content/uploads/sites/2/2020/06/Salo_imagoesite_2019_ENG_web.pdf

Wheeler, A. (2023, August 11). 9 Things You Need To Know Before Visiting Finland - A Globe Well Travelled. A Globe Well Travelled. https://www.aglobewelltravelled.com/2023/08/11/9-things-you-need-to-know-before-visiting-finland/

www.thingstodopost.org. (2018, March 16). What to Do and See in Northern Ostrobothnia, Finland: The Best Places and Tips. Things to Do. https://www.thingstodopost.org/what-to-do-and-see-in-northern-ostrobothnia-finland-the-best-places-and-tips-122886

Image Sources

[1] *TUBS, CC BY-SA 3.0 <https://creativecommons.org/licenses/by-sa/3.0>, via Wikimedia Commons: https://commons.wikimedia.org/wiki/File:Lappi_in_Finland.svg*

[2] *JRC, EC, CC BY 4.0 <https://creativecommons.org/licenses/by/4.0>, via Wikimedia Commons https://commons.wikimedia.org/wiki/File:Finland_Base_map.png*

[3] *Simo Räsänen, CC BY-SA 4.0 <https://creativecommons.org/licenses/by-sa/4.0>, via Wikimedia Commons. https://commons.wikimedia.org/wiki/File:Winter_at_J%C3%A4niskoski_in_Inari,_Lapland,_Finland,_2018_March.jpg*

[4] *https://commons.wikimedia.org/wiki/File:Albert_Edelfelt-Sj%C3%A4lvportr%C3%A4tt.jpg*

[5] *Tiia Monto, CC BY-SA 4.0 <https://creativecommons.org/licenses/by-sa/4.0>, via Wikimedia Commons. https://commons.wikimedia.org/wiki/File:Tampere_Orthodox_Church_2019.jpg*

[6] *Simo Räsänen, CC BY-SA 4.0 <https://creativecommons.org/licenses/by-sa/4.0>, via Wikimedia Commons. https://commons.wikimedia.org/wiki/File:Crowds_gathered_around_Havis_Amanda_statue_after_the_championship_gold_in_ice_hockey_in_Kaartinkaupunki,_Helsinki,_Finland,_2022_May_-_2.jpg*

[7] *Ralf Roletschek, GFDL 1.2 <http://www.gnu.org/licenses/old-licenses/fdl-1.2.html>, via Wikimedia Commons. https://commons.wikimedia.org/wiki/File:15-12-20-Helsinki-Vantaan-Lentoasema-N3S_3110.jpg*

[8] *OpenStreetMap Contributors: openstreetmap.org*

[9] *John Samuel, CC BY-SA 4.0 <https://creativecommons.org/licenses/by-sa/4.0>, via Wikimedia Commons. https://commons.wikimedia.org/wiki/File:Helsinki_Cathedral_view.jpg*

[10] *https://pixabay.com/photos/architecture-helsinki-senate-square-3435487/*

[11] *FoxyStranger Kawasaki, CC BY-SA 3.0 <https://creativecommons.org/licenses/by-sa/3.0>, via Wikimedia Commons. https://commons.wikimedia.org/wiki/File:Suomenlinna_Sea_Fortress_-_panoramio.jpg*

[12] *Old Pionear, CC BY-SA 4.0 <https://creativecommons.org/licenses/by-sa/4.0>, via Wikimedia Commons. https://commons.wikimedia.org/wiki/File:Temppeliaukio_Church_(sis%C3%A4puolelta).jpg*

[13] *Finnish National Gallery, CC BY-SA 4.0 <https://creativecommons.org/licenses/by-sa/4.0>, via Wikimedia Commons. https://commons.wikimedia.org/wiki/File:Art_museum_Ateneum_in_Kluuvi,_Helsinki,_Finland,_2014.jpg*

[14] *Aulo Aasmaa, CC BY 3.0 <https://creativecommons.org/licenses/by/3.0>, via Wikimedia Commons. https://commons.wikimedia.org/wiki/File:Kiasma_-_Museum_of_Modern_Art_-_panoramio.jpg*

[15] *I99pema, CC BY-SA 4.0 <https://creativecommons.org/licenses/by-sa/4.0>, via Wikimedia Commons. https://commons.wikimedia.org/wiki/File:Finnish_National_Theatre,_Helsinki.jpg*

[16] *Diego Delso, CC BY-SA 3.0 <https://creativecommons.org/licenses/by-sa/3.0>, via Wikimedia*

Commons. https://commons.wikimedia.org/wiki/File:Centro_Musical_de_Helsinki_, Finlandia,_2012-08-14,_DD_01.JPG

[17] Lauren Stevens, CC BY-SA 4.0 <https://creativecommons.org/licenses/by-sa/4.0>, via Wikimedia Commons. https://commons.wikimedia.org/wiki/File:Helsinki_Design_Museum_on_4th_April_2015.jpg

[18] Ximonic (Simo Räsänen), CC BY-SA 3.0 <https://creativecommons.org/licenses/by-sa/3.0>, via Wikimedia Commons. https://commons.wikimedia.org/wiki/File:Myyras_in_western_Sipoo,_Uusimaa,_Finland,_2021_March.jpg

[19] Samoasambia, CC BY-SA 3.0 <https://creativecommons.org/licenses/by-sa/3.0>, via Wikimedia Commons. https://commons.wikimedia.org/wiki/File:View_from_Kirkonsalmi_bridge,_Naantali_2013.JPG

[20] Ximonic, Simo Räsänen, GFDL <http://www.gnu.org/copyleft/fdl.html>, via Wikimedia Commons: https://commons.wikimedia.org/wiki/File:Ympyrk%C3%A4inenlampi_in_Nuuksio_National_Park_2.jpg

[21] JIP at English Wikipedia, CC BY-SA 3.0 <https://creativecommons.org/licenses/by-sa/3.0>, via Wikimedia Commons. https://commons.wikimedia.org/wiki/File:EMMA_from_outside.jpg

[22] Simo Räsänen, CC BY 4.0 <https://creativecommons.org/licenses/by/4.0>, via Wikimedia Commons. https://commons.wikimedia.org/wiki/File:Science_centre_Heureka_in_Tikkurila,_Vantaa,_Finland,_2022_June.jpg

[23] Ximonic (Simo Räsänen), CC BY 3.0 <https://creativecommons.org/licenses/by/3.0>, via Wikimedia Commons: https://commons.wikimedia.org/wiki/File:Church_of_St._Lawrence_from_west_in_Helsingin_Pit%C3%A4j%C3%A4n_Kirkonkyl%C3%A4,_Vantaa,_Finland,_2021_July.jpg

[24] Havu Pellikka, CC BY-SA 4.0 <https://creativecommons.org/licenses/by-sa/4.0>, via Wikimedia Commons. https://commons.wikimedia.org/wiki/File:Porvoo_Cathedral_and_old_town_Dec_2017.jpg

[25] Havu Pellikka, CC BY-SA 4.0 <https://creativecommons.org/licenses/by-sa/4.0>, via Wikimedia Commons. https://commons.wikimedia.org/wiki/File:Porvoo_cathedral_bell_tower_Dec_2017.jpg

[26] Nemo bis, CC BY-SA 4.0 <https://creativecommons.org/licenses/by-sa/4.0>, via Wikimedia Commons. https://commons.wikimedia.org/wiki/File:Porvoo_-_Porvoo_Museum_-_20180819130538.jpg

[27] Antti Bilund, CC BY-SA 3.0 <https://creativecommons.org/licenses/by-sa/3.0>, via Wikimedia Commons. https://commons.wikimedia.org/wiki/File:Kirkkonummi_church_1_AB.jpg

[28] Ullake, CC BY-SA 4.0 <https://creativecommons.org/licenses/by-sa/4.0>, via Wikimedia Commons. https://commons.wikimedia.org/wiki/File:Hvittr%C3%A4sk_summer.jpg

[29] dr.eros, CC BY 3.0 <https://creativecommons.org/licenses/by/3.0>, via Wikimedia Commons. https://commons.wikimedia.org/wiki/File:Loviisa_fortress_-_panoramio.jpg

[30] Outdoors Finland, CC BY 2.0 <https://creativecommons.org/licenses/by/2.0>, via Wikimedia Commons. https://commons.wikimedia.org/wiki/File:Kalkkiruukin_laavu,_a_lean-to_in_Sipoonkorpi_National_Park,_2013.jpg

[31] *MrFinland, CC BY-SA 3.0 <https://creativecommons.org/licenses/by-sa/3.0>, via Wikimedia Commons. https://commons.wikimedia.org/wiki/File:Sipoo_Old_Church_2009.JPG*

[32] *User: (WT-shared) Aiko99ann at wts wikivoyage, CC BY-SA 4.0 <https://creativecommons.org/licenses/by-sa/4.0>, via Wikimedia Commons: https://commons.wikimedia.org/wiki/File:Naantali_oldtown_01.jpg*

[33] *https://commons.wikimedia.org/wiki/File:Naantali_1920-luvulla.jpg*

[34] *TUBS, CC BY-SA 3.0 <https://creativecommons.org/licenses/by-sa/3.0>, via Wikimedia Commons. https://commons.wikimedia.org/wiki/File:Lappi_in_Finland.svg*

[35] *Ninara, CC BY 2.0 <https://creativecommons.org/licenses/by/2.0>, via Wikimedia Commons. https://commons.wikimedia.org/wiki/File:Lake_Kilpisj%C3%A4rvi_in_Enonteki%C3%B6,_Lapland,_Finland,_2021_September.jpg*

[36] *Manfred Werner - Tsui, CC BY-SA 3.0 <https://creativecommons.org/licenses/by-sa/3.0>, via Wikimedia Commons. https://commons.wikimedia.org/wiki/File:SIIDA_Inari,_Suomi_Finland_2013-03-10_001.jpg*

[37] *Francisco M. Marzoa Alonso, CC BY-SA 2.5 <https://creativecommons.org/licenses/by-sa/2.5>, via Wikimedia Commons. https://commons.wikimedia.org/wiki/File:BoatInari1.jpg*

[38] *Pinterest, CC BY-SA 3.0 <https://creativecommons.org/licenses/by-sa/3.0>, via Wikimedia Commons. https://commons.wikimedia.org/wiki/File:Northern_Lights,_Alena_Aenami.png*

[39] *EerikLehto, CC BY-SA 4.0 <https://creativecommons.org/licenses/by-sa/4.0>, via Wikimedia Commons: https://commons.wikimedia.org/wiki/File:The_old_church_of_Sodankyl%C3%A4.jpg*

[40] *Art of Backpacking, CC BY 2.0 <https://creativecommons.org/licenses/by/2.0>, via Wikimedia Commons. https://commons.wikimedia.org/wiki/File:SnowCastle,_Kemi,_Finland.jpg*

[41] *Estormiz, CC0, via Wikimedia Commons. https://commons.wikimedia.org/wiki/File:Kemi_Gemstone_Gallery_20070808.JPG*

[42] *Simo Räsänen, CC BY-SA 4.0 <https://creativecommons.org/licenses/by-sa/4.0>, via Wikimedia Commons. https://commons.wikimedia.org/wiki/File:Naapurinvaara_in_Sotkamo,_Kainuu,_Finland,_2022_August_-_2.jpg*

[43] *Fenn-O-maniC, CC BY-SA 3.0 <https://creativecommons.org/licenses/by-sa/3.0>, via Wikimedia Commons. https://commons.wikimedia.org/wiki/File:Kainuu_sijainti_Suomi.svg*

[44] *Jniemenmaa, CC BY-SA 3.0 <http://creativecommons.org/licenses/by-sa/3.0/>, via Wikimedia Commons. https://commons.wikimedia.org/wiki/File:Karelia_today.png*

[45] *Estormiz, CC0, via Wikimedia Commons: https://commons.wikimedia.org/wiki/File:Kajaani_Castle_Ruins_20210421_01.jpg*

[46] *https://commons.wikimedia.org/wiki/File:Ouluj%C3%A4rvi_Paltaselk%C3%A4.JPG*

[47] *Tomisti, CC BY-SA 4.0 <https://creativecommons.org/licenses/by-sa/4.0>, via Wikimedia Commons: https://commons.wikimedia.org/wiki/File:Joensuu_Art_Museum.jpg*

[48] *Pertsaboy, CC BY-SA 3.0 <http://creativecommons.org/licenses/by-sa/3.0/>, via Wikimedia Commons https://commons.wikimedia.org/wiki/File:New_Valamo_monastery_main_church,_summer.jpg*

[49] 5snake5, CC0, via Wikimedia Commons: https://commons.wikimedia.org/wiki/File:Sunset_at_Sainaa_Lake.jpg

[50] TUBS, CC BY-SA 3.0 <https://creativecommons.org/licenses/by-sa/3.0>, via Wikimedia Commons. https://commons.wikimedia.org/wiki/File:Pohjois-Savo_sijainti_Suomi.svg

[51] TUBS, CC BY-SA 3.0 <https://creativecommons.org/licenses/by-sa/3.0>, via Wikimedia Commons. https://commons.wikimedia.org/wiki/File:Etel%C3%A4-Savo_in_Finland.svg

[52] Tiia Monto, CC BY-SA 3.0 <https://creativecommons.org/licenses/by-sa/3.0>, via Wikimedia Commons: https://commons.wikimedia.org/wiki/File:Puijo_tower.jpg

[53] Koothe, CC BY-SA 4.0 <https://creativecommons.org/licenses/by-sa/4.0>, via Wikimedia Commons: https://commons.wikimedia.org/wiki/File:Olavinlinna_2016_1.jpg

[54] Sino Yu, CC BY-SA 4.0 <https://creativecommons.org/licenses/by-sa/4.0>, via Wikimedia Commons: https://commons.wikimedia.org/wiki/File:Linnansaari_National_Park_20130806_04.jpg

[55] Attribution-ShareAlike 3.0 Unported, CC BY-SA 3.0 <https://creativecommons.org/licenses/by-sa/3.0/deed.en> https://commons.wikimedia.org/wiki/File:Mikkeli_Cathedral.jpg

[56] Ohto Kokko, CC BY-SA 3.0 <http://creativecommons.org/licenses/by-sa/3.0/>, via Wikimedia Commons: https://commons.wikimedia.org/wiki/File:Astuvansalmi_hirvia.jpg

[57] Paju ~commonswiki, CC BY-SA 3.0 <https://creativecommons.org/licenses/by-sa/3.0>, via Wikimedia Commons: https://commons.wikimedia.org/wiki/File:Mekaanisen_musiikin_museo_-_Pelimanninkatu_8_-_78850_Varkaus.jpg

[58] Fenn-O-maniC, CC BY-SA 3.0 <https://creativecommons.org/licenses/by-sa/3.0>, via Wikimedia Commons https://commons.wikimedia.org/wiki/File:Keski-Suomi_sijainti_Suomi.svg

[59] Tiia Monto, CC BY-SA 4.0 <https://creativecommons.org/licenses/by-sa/4.0>, via Wikimedia Commons: https://commons.wikimedia.org/wiki/File:Alvar_Aalto_museum_2017.jpg

[60] Tiia Monto, CC BY-SA 3.0 <https://creativecommons.org/licenses/by-sa/3.0>, via Wikimedia Commons: https://commons.wikimedia.org/wiki/File:Pyh%C3%A4-H%C3%A4kki_National_Park_5.jpg

[61] Santtu37, CC BY-SA 4.0 <https://creativecommons.org/licenses/by-sa/4.0>, via Wikimedia Commons: https://commons.wikimedia.org/wiki/File:Saarij%C3%A4rvi_j%C3%A4rvi.jpg

[62] Santeri Viinamäki, CC BY-SA 4.0 <https://creativecommons.org/licenses/by-sa/4.0>, via Wikimedia Commons: https://commons.wikimedia.org/wiki/File:Keuruu_Museum_20210628.jpg

[63] https://commons.wikimedia.org/wiki/File:Pihlajaveden-kirkko-2.jpg

[64] Fenn-O-maniC, CC BY-SA 3.0 <https://creativecommons.org/licenses/by-sa/3.0>, via Wikimedia Commons. https://commons.wikimedia.org/wiki/File:Pohjanmaa_sijainti_Suomi.svg

[65] PtG, CC BY-SA 4.0 <https://creativecommons.org/licenses/by-sa/4.0>, via Wikimedia Commons: https://commons.wikimedia.org/wiki/File:Vaasa_maritime_museum.jpg

[66] Fenn-O-maniC, CC BY-SA 3.0 <https://creativecommons.org/licenses/by-sa/3.0>, via Wikimedia Commons: https://commons.wikimedia.org/wiki/File:Sein%C3%A4joki_sijainti_Suomi.svg

[67] kallerna, CC BY-SA 4.0 <https://creativecommons.org/licenses/by-sa/4.0>, via Wikimedia

Commons: https://commons.wikimedia.org/wiki/File:Lakeuden_risti_2021_3.jpg

[68] Fenn-O-maniC, CC BY-SA 3.0 <https://creativecommons.org/licenses/by-sa/3.0>, via Wikimedia Commons: https://commons.wikimedia.org/wiki/File:Kokkola_sijainti_Suomi.svg

[69] Jukka Kolppanen, CC BY-SA 3.0 <https://creativecommons.org/licenses/by-sa/3.0>, via Wikimedia Commons: https://commons.wikimedia.org/wiki/File:K.H._Renlundin_museo.jpg

[70] Fenn-O-maniC, CC BY-SA 3.0 <https://creativecommons.org/licenses/by-sa/3.0>, via Wikimedia Commons: https://commons.wikimedia.org/wiki/File:Oulu_sijainti_Suomi.svg

[71] Estormiz, CC0, via Wikimedia Commons: https://commons.wikimedia.org/wiki/File:Nallikari_Oulu_20130811_02.JPG

[72] Fenn-O-maniC, CC BY-SA 3.0 <https://creativecommons.org/licenses/by-sa/3.0>, via Wikimedia Commons: https://commons.wikimedia.org/wiki/File:Raahe_sijainti_Suomi.svg

[73] Estormiz, CC0, via Wikimedia Commons: https://commons.wikimedia.org/wiki/File:Raahe_Museum_20210426.jpg

[74] https://pixabay.com/photos/lake-trees-sunset-sun-sunlight-1365288/

[75] OpenStreetMap Contributors: openstreetmap.org

[76] OpenStreetMap Contributors: openstreetmap.org

[77] OpenStreetMap Contributors: openstreetmap.org

[78] OpenStreetMap Contributors: openstreetmap.org

[79] OpenStreetMap Contributors: openstreetmap.org

[80] OpenStreetMap Contributors: openstreetmap.org

[81] OpenStreetMap Contributors: openstreetmap.org

[82] OpenStreetMap Contributors: openstreetmap.org

[83] OpenStreetMap Contributors: openstreetmap.org

[84] OpenStreetMap Contributors: openstreetmap.org

[85] OpenStreetMap Contributors: openstreetmap.org

[86] OpenStreetMap Contributors: openstreetmap.org

[87] OpenStreetMap Contributors: openstreetmap.org

[88] OpenStreetMap Contributors: openstreetmap.org

[89] OpenStreetMap Contributors: openstreetmap.org

[90] OpenStreetMap Contributors: openstreetmap.org

[91] OpenStreetMap Contributors: openstreetmap.org

[92] OpenStreetMap Contributors: openstreetmap.org

[93] OpenStreetMap Contributors: openstreetmap.org

[94] OpenStreetMap Contributors: openstreetmap.org

[95] https://www.pexels.com/photo/nature-sunny-holiday-love-8531226/

72690996R00118